TEACHING ETHICS IN SCHOOLS

TEACHING ETHICS IN SCHOOLS

A new
approach
to moral
education

PHILIP CAM

ACER PRESS

First published 2012
by ACER Press, an imprint of
Australian Council *for* Educational Research Ltd
19 Prospect Hill Road, Camberwell
Victoria, 3124, Australia

www.acerpress.com.au
sales@acer.edu.au

Text copyright © Philip Cam 2012
Design and typography copyright © ACER Press 2012

Edited by Elisa Webb
Cover design, text design and typesetting by ACER Project Publishing
Printed in Australia by BPA Print Group

National Library of Australia Cataloguing-in-Publication entry:
Author: Cam, Philip, 1948-
Title: Teaching ethics in schools : a new approach to
               moral education / Philip Cam.
ISBN: 9781742860633 (pbk.)
Notes: Includes bibliographical references.
Subjects: Moral education.
               Education--Philosophy.
               Ethics.
Dewey Number: 370.114

CONTENTS

INTRODUCTION

The problem of moral education

In my grandparents' generation there was a widespread belief that 'to spare the rod is to spoil the child'. Although this attitude was already on the wane when I was young, my father was still liable to inflict corporal punishment for misdemeanours, as were some of my teachers. They believed that it was the way to bring up children to be of good character and to do what is right. No doubt some parents still follow that tradition today, although societal rejection of it has become widespread and the use of corporal punishment in the classroom is not tolerated. Changing approaches to moral education are accompanied by changes in moral beliefs and attitudes themselves. To take an obvious example relating to adults, attitudes towards de facto relationships are very different today than when I was growing up. We have only to look back at law reform in this area to acknowledge a shift in community attitudes. This raises obvious problems for moral education. We want our children to develop a strong sense of values and to learn to make the right ethical decisions. Yet how are schools to navigate such waters, given the crosswinds and shifting currents facing moral education?

The home and the school

One response to this problem is to say that schools should leave moral education to the home; it should be left to parents to instil their own values in their children. This does not mean that schools should altogether wash their hands of moral matters. They have plenty to be getting on with, in seeing that students obey school rules, dealing with obvious moral transgressions and the righting of wrongs that occur in the playground and classroom. But they should steer clear of anything that might be a source of contention with parents. And they certainly should not touch upon areas of moral debate in the wider community.

As sensible as such a policy may sound, it comes at a price. We must face the fact that the home is not necessarily the cradle we wish it to be. We can always blame parents in cases of bad example or moral neglect, but what good does recrimination do us when society has to pick up the pieces? Quarantining moral education inside the home makes no attempt to provide the educational means of helping society to deal with moral disagreement and uncertainty. Through something akin to a sin of omission, it allows such tensions and divisions to replicate without providing students with the moral means of sorting them out. Although there is probably no prescription for moral education that apportions responsibility between the school and the home to everyone's satisfaction, the most reasonable course of action is to try to accommodate these interests by forming a partnership—one in which the school avoids encroachment upon the rights of parents to bring up their children in the values of the home, while striving to augment them. In doing this, we need to acknowledge that the moral domain is a source of disagreement and debate and to help students to learn how to deal with that productively.

The appeal to religion

Another approach to moral education is to appeal to religion. Religious people look to their faith for moral guidance, and children brought up within a faith are introduced to its moral teachings. This occurs in the home as well as within the religious community, and is embedded in children's educational experience if they attend a faith-based school.

Although the vast majority of Australians identify with one or another religious faith, this is often only nominal and it would be a mistake to think that children in those families are necessarily brought up within a faith-based morality. So far as schooling is concerned, two-thirds of children attend government schools, where a growing number of them have little or no direct contact with religion. Whatever value a religiously based morality may have for one sector of society, it is bound to fall on deaf ears or meet with vigorous rejection in other quarters. It is therefore in no position to meet the general need for moral education in non-religious schools.

While this points to the need for a secular intervention, it is sometimes claimed that morality cannot be separated from religion. The implication is that children brought up without religion either lack true morality, or that any morality they do have originates from a religion of which they are otherwise deprived. This view exaggerates the role of religion in the historical and cultural mix that informs morality. Moral precepts and understandings derive as much from philosophical traditions as from religious ones. For instance, some version of the Golden Rule—treat others as you wish to be treated—is a feature of almost all philosophical ethical traditions, both ancient and modern. Some of the most famous of the Christian church fathers such as St Augustine and St Thomas Aquinas were influenced by Western philosophers like Plato and Aristotle. Religious and philosophical systems have often been intertwined, religion having benefited from philosophy as well as inspired it.

Turning to philosophy

I make this point not only to counter the claim that morality must derive from religion, but also to suggest that philosophy provides a source of thought about moral matters that is of value to school education. Ethics is a branch of philosophy that has been taught within higher educational institutions since classical antiquity, and there is no reason why it should not be adapted for use in schools. As with the other disciplines that students first meet at school, a suitably framed introduction to ethics can be introduced from the early years, not only as a subject worthy of study in its own right, but as an aspect of study throughout the curriculum.

To place moral education firmly within the curriculum is quite different from regarding it as an aspect of behaviour management, or as a matter of exhortation. Even so, to treat moral education as an extension of the curriculum is not to see it as being divorced from conduct—no area of the curriculum should be like that. On the contrary, an appropriately structured ethics program may be expected to have a highly beneficial effect upon both the conduct and the character of students—and insofar as it is integrated into their studies, upon the whole tenor of their education.

Avoiding both relativism and absolutism

The home and the church can be sources of moral authority in a way that our government schools cannot. This stems from the fact that government schools gather together children from all kinds of social and religious backgrounds, and their attempts to impress a common set of values upon a diverse population of students can clash with the tendency to treat values as culturally or even individually relative.

Cultural relativism can arise through the recognition and celebration of the multicultural nature of our society, coupled with an insistence that all of the different religious or ethnic beliefs and practices should be honoured. In its individualistic form, relativism has gained succour from constructivism, an influential learning theory according to which students learn by constructing their own representations and beliefs. By a somewhat slippery inference, constructivism is sometimes taken to imply that what is good or right for one person may not be so for another, making values relative to the individual. While it is difficult to square cultural relativism with individualistic relativism, both are alive and well in our schools.

In contradistinction to this plurality of values in government schools, an acceptance of the relativity of values does not often sit well with religious and cultural values themselves. Many people in the different social or ethnic groups that make up our society tend to look askance at ways of life at variance to their own, often viewing them with mistrust and occasionally with hostility. Nor do the various faiths normally regard their own beliefs and values as only true or right for them. While relativism is meant to be accommodating, it can encourage scepticism toward the very idea of having the right beliefs and values—if any group's beliefs and values are truly as acceptable as any other, then one set of beliefs and values is as good as another, including your own. Individualistic relativism fares even worse. If what is true and right is only true and right *for me*, then there isn't any point in discussing whether I am in error, provided that I remain true to myself—whatever that may mean. Beyond that, the business of moral evaluation simply evaporates.

The fact that students come from a variety of backgrounds does require attention, but the relativist response goes astray. Its anti-judgmental policy is the opposite extreme of an absolutism which says that there is one true or correct view and it is mine (or ours), and anything else is untrue or immoral. We need an approach to moral education that will enable us to navigate between the extremes of absolutism and relativism. In this regard it is important to note that neither of these hazards is friendly to the idea of moral questioning and debate. One stands for unquestionable moral authority in absolute terms, while the other makes morality individually subjective or rests moral authority in the settled opinions and values of the group. The alternative to both views is to encourage discussion and thoughtful deliberation about beliefs and values. A satisfactory approach to moral education in an open society should set that course.

Developing good moral judgment

The history of opinion regarding the moral makeup of children has witnessed no more vividly contrasting views than the puritan belief that children are born in sin, and the romantic conception of childhood innocence. The former had it that childish disobedience is a sign of the devil, to be driven out by discipline and punishment, while the latter maintained that society corrupts children and robs them of their natural virtue. Both notions are erroneous. One was based on the pernicious myth of a fully-formed and malevolent agent acting within or through the child. The other mistook inexperience and nascent personal formation for goodness, and combined this naïve conception of childhood with a jaundiced view of society. While young children are obviously capable of being good or being naughty on occasion, the fact is that they do not yet have a fully developed capacity for moral judgment. This means that moral education is not a matter of rooting out what is inherently evil or of preserving children's angelic virtue, but of helping them to acquire good moral judgment.

Consideration of a more familiar opinion can be used to make the same point. No special provision would need to be made for moral education if any right-minded person always knew what to think or do, morally speaking. In that case, we would simply need to encourage children to do the right thing and correct them when they do not. While this is a commonly held view, and it is true that children, like the rest of us, do need moral encouragement and correction on occasion, the idea that the right and the good are always settled in advance misrepresents the nature of most moral difficulties. It conceives of them as conflicts between good and evil, or right and wrong, where we are tempted to do what we already know we should not do because of moral weakness or the pressure of circumstance. While there are such occasions, moral problems and issues far more commonly involve having to decide between competing goods or choosing the lesser of evils. Here it is often entirely possible for two reasonable people who are acquainted with all the relevant considerations to come to different conclusions. Should I put less effort into my career in order to spend more time with my family? Should I keep my promise on this occasion even if it may result in harm? Should I tell her the truth even though it may hurt her feelings? There can be no overriding presumption that a right-minded person will automatically know what to do in many such cases. They call for deliberation and judgment.

Good moral judgment is not something that we can expect to develop automatically. The most casual survey of our fellows undermines the suggestion that none of us is in need of any training in this regard, and this is certainly no less so when it comes to children. The development of good moral judgment takes time and effort, and benefits from a working knowledge of what is at stake in various ways of forming such judgments. This is a task for moral education, and, more particularly, for the kind of exploration that occurs in ethics.

Teaching ethics through collaborative inquiry

Since ethics is a branch of philosophy, the key to success in teaching it is to engage students philosophically, which involves reasoned inquiry into issues and ideas. It may be as elementary as learning to distinguish between moral and non-moral uses of a word such as 'good', or as advanced as determining whether the consequences of a given action are more (or less) morally significant than the intention with which a person acted. At any level, there is a vital difference between teaching ethics through inquiry and teaching it didactically. The latter gives students much to learn but little to reflect upon. The former shifts the emphasis from telling students what they should think about moral matters to helping them to think morally. Moreover, ethical inquiry gives students ways of thinking about such matters that they could hardly obtain otherwise. Through ethical inquiry, they learn to think as ethicists have thought, and to apply that thinking to all kinds of problems and issues. In other words, they learn to do what ethicists have done rather than simply learning what ethicists have said.

Even so, it makes a very great difference whether ethical inquiry is carried out as a personal exploration or in collaboration with others. Consider something as common as two people taking different sides on an ethical issue. One blames an individual for a given transgression, say, while the other faults society for having done little or nothing about the conditions that the individual has had to endure. Both judgments may have merit as well as limitations—in which case the protagonists have something to learn from one another. Let us suppose that our protagonists approach this matter in the spirit of collaborative inquiry. In hearing each other out, they are led to reflect on each other's opinions and have their attention drawn to morally relevant considerations that they may have overlooked or to a different assessment of their significance. By engaging in the give-and-take of reasons with one another, they submit their respective judgments to analysis and evidence. And by becoming prepared to consider each other's viewpoints, they learn to be more reasonable in their dealings with one another. This repertoire of practice is itself a form of ethical conduct. It shows thoughtfulness, respect, due consideration and moderation. That makes it an ideal vehicle for moral education.

The collaborative ethical inquiry approach to moral education is highly versatile and able to be employed from the early years as well as embedded in a range of school subjects. This means that it is a platform upon which to build a systematic approach to moral education—one in which students' ethical knowledge and understanding can be developed over the years and in which the moral aspects of their studies receive regular attention.

The approach also avoids the mistake of treating students as moral beings so far as their social conduct is concerned and as amoral intellects in regard to academic matters. It allows us to engage students in the moral consideration of issues and ideas that are relevant to their studies. In assisting them to investigate the ethical implications of what they are learning, it treats students as whole human beings, whose attitudes and affections are as much a matter for educational concern as their intellectual knowledge and understanding. Nothing less should be expected if we are truly to treat students as persons.

About the book

Teaching ethics in schools is in two parts; the first section deals with the theoretical base on which successful moral education must be based, while the second contains practical strategies and exercises that may be used as stimulus material for teachers in schools.

Chapter 1 introduces things that we need to consider as we begin to think about moral education. First, we need to have a clear idea of what we are talking about when we refer to morality. My approach will be to characterise it in terms of the nature of moral judgment, something that will turn out to be of the greatest importance as we proceed. In addition to the nature of morality, there are questions about its origin or source, whether social, natural or religious, as well as about the capacities upon which its exercise depends. We also need to think about the beginnings of children's moral life before they attend school and the development of their moral experience outside of the classroom during the school years. These are conditions that any scheme of moral education must recognise and build upon. They inevitably mean that children will bring different beliefs and opinions into the classroom, and we need to find productive ways of acknowledging this. Finally, it is important to think about moral education within a broad conception of the kind of society for which we are trying to educate. It is one thing to say that we believe in an open and democratic society and quite another to ensure that we educate for one. Nowhere is a tension between democratic objectives and actual practice more likely than when it comes to moral education.

Chapter 2 begins with a critical appraisal of conventional approaches to moral education. Included in this is traditional moral instruction, uses of rewards and punishments and character training. While these approaches have their place, space needs to be created for an approach that is more in keeping with contemporary educational objectives. We need to shift the emphasis from telling students *what* to think to teaching them *how* to think about moral matters. This is where philosophy comes in. The way to develop good moral judgment is by using the tools of philosophy to explore ethics through collaborative inquiry. This area of philosophy need be in no way formidable and can readily be incorporated into many areas of the curriculum across the school years.

Chapter 3 provides an easy-reading introduction to ethics. While you do not need an extensive knowledge of this area of philosophy in order to appreciate what is involved in an ethics-based approach to moral education, it is necessary to have a basic understanding of the field. An introduction to some of the core ideas of philosophers such as Aristotle, Kant and Mill is provided, together with discussion of the different kinds of theories that are meant to provide a basis for moral judgment and the kinds of justification that may be given of those theories. Also included is an exploration of the moral use of terms such as 'good' and 'right', an examination of the basis of morality, the sources of moral knowledge and conditions of moral responsibility.

Chapter 4 introduces the second part of the book by showing you how to use collaborative inquiry in order to teach ethics. This approach makes frequent use of discussion. While most teachers are familiar with discussion-based workgroups, oral student presentations or engaging students in class discussion or debate, not all will have experienced collaborative inquiry, with its emphasis on dialogue, on students questioning one another, on testing out one another's opinions and exploring the implications of different suggestions and ideas. Guidance will therefore be given to help make a success of this kind of work in the classroom, including everything from basic tips about classroom setup and choosing appropriate stimulus material, to how to develop students' powers of questioning, conceptual exploration and reasoning.

Chapter 5 provides teachers with further background for teaching ethics and shows you how to construct exercises and activities for the classroom. This includes activities that will help you to stimulate and structure class discussion, as well as work carried out in pairs and small groups. In a book such as this, I obviously cannot hope to provide materials for a whole range of subject areas across all the years of schooling. That is neither feasible nor appropriate. My aim is to set you on the road to success in constructing materials that will assist in such aspects of inquiry as questioning, conceptual exploration and reasoning. I hope to encourage you to work with your colleagues to explore the ethical aspects of the material that you teach and to find ways to make what you discover accessible to students through discussion and activities that follow the principles and practices laid down.

After many years of working with teachers in this and related fields, I am confident that any teacher who is determined to make a success of using collaborative inquiry in the classroom will not be disappointed. I am also convinced of the considerable merits of this approach when it comes to contemporary moral education. It is now my task to show you that these claims are true—that in both theory and practice, the ethical approach to moral education is the way forward.

PART ONE

CHAPTER 1

The background to moral education

The moral domain

What is morality? We are so familiar with moral approval and condemnation that this may seem an odd question to ask. All the more so for teachers who regularly attend to the conduct of students, praising their good behaviour and reprimanding them for misdemeanours. Not all commendation or reproach has a moral character, of course. The student whose sporting prowess is applauded or one whose untidy handwriting is lamented is not being subjected to moral appraisal. Even so, it is not all that obvious where non-moral judgment leaves off and moral judgment begins. That is as good an indication as any that we had better make an attempt to be clear about what we mean by morality before we launch into a discussion of moral education.

It might be said that moral judgments have to do with the difference between good and bad, or right and wrong. The trouble is that these terms also have non-moral uses. While we talk about doing good deeds, or think that someone has been a bad influence, or try to do the right thing and condemn wrongdoing, we also speak of a good work-out or a bad cold, about getting the right answer in maths, or getting off the bus at the wrong stop. So, to say that morality has to do with good and bad, right and wrong, is not sufficient to define it.

Let's begin with an obvious point. To complain that the weather is bad is clearly not to make a moral judgment. Moral judgments apply only to people—or, at least, to what we may call *agents*. By an agent, I mean an individual or party capable of acting with an intention, or of doing something on purpose. The weather may be bad, but it is not deliberately behaving that way. It is not an agent that can do things on purpose. The same can be said of character traits. The weather in Tierra del Fuego may be characteristically bad, but it cannot be of bad character, like an agent.

Moral judgments are restricted to the rights and wrongs of the conduct of agents, or to evaluations of their motivation or character. Yet this is still not sufficient to ensure that we are dealing with moral judgment. An undertaking may be poorly motivated simply because it is ill-considered. Conduct may go astray because of ignorance or faulty reckoning. An aspect of a person's make-up may be irritating without being deemed a moral failing. We would not say the same of behaviour that is deliberately designed to be injurious, however, or of conduct motivated by unbridled self-interest or contempt for the welfare of others. We would not say it of callousness, spitefulness, meanness or similar qualities of character. Why not? One thing that the latter have in common is their connection with wilful harm or disregard of the consequences of action—with deliberately harmful conduct; motivation that pays no heed to the damage done to others; or character that displays itself in unabashedly harsh and hurtful ways. Such things contrast with attempts to relieve suffering; actions motivated by a desire to promote the general welfare; and character traits that show themselves in kindness and compassion. This suggests that intended or foreseeable benefit or harm flowing from character and conduct are relevant to moral judgment.

For reasons that will eventually become apparent, it cannot be claimed that the above considerations lead to an unobjectionable definition of the moral domain. But they will do for present purposes. We may say that the moral domain is one in which the conduct of agents is evaluated in terms of the benefit or harm intended, or that should have been foreseen, and the good or ill associated with various motivations and traits of character.

The origin of and capacity for morality

Two related issues regarding the moral domain need to be disentangled. One has to do with where morality comes from and the other with the capacities upon which it depends. Morality may be thought of as handed down from God, for example, or taken to be a product of natural evolution, or supposed to emerge from the history of social arrangements. So far as our capacities are concerned, morality may be taken to depend upon, among other things, our ability to reason; the disposition of the will; natural sympathies that gain expression as concern and care for one another; or a conscience implanted in us.

There is no simple correspondence between views about the origin of morality and claims about the capacities upon which it is supposed to depend. Conjectures as to whether the origin of morality is transcendent, biological or social may be variously combined with conceptions of the capacities upon which it may be supposed to depend. The idea of conscience may be construed as a specially created capacity for insight into God's law, for instance, or considered to be some naturally evolved mechanism that resolves competing impulses, or thought of as an internalisation of the prohibitions of the parent arising in early childhood. Expressions of sympathy may be seen as an evolutionary strategy that confers selective advantage, as manifesting God's law written into our hearts, or as part of a means of maintaining social norms through a system of recompenses and withholdings.

This is not the place to attempt to sort through these complexities. Even so, questions about the origins of morality and the capacities upon which it depends should be kept in mind as we begin to think about how best to approach the topic of moral education.

The beginnings of moral experience

Infants are agents that have needs and capacities. To speak of infants as agents is to acknowledge that their behaviour is not simply a function of external factors operating upon them. The ongoing activity of infants is driven by their own capacities and needs. Here lie the seeds of their exploratory behaviour. The ability to grasp something and bring it to the mouth is not merely a way of satisfying bodily needs by feeding. Combined with the infant's native curiosity, it also satisfies the needs of elementary inquiry into things at hand. When infants begin to crawl—and later to walk—the range of their activities increases. There is curiosity about all manner of objects. Far from being passive recipients of environmental stimulation, young children are creators, explorers and experimenters. That's how they make sense of their world.

Of course, the infant's attempts to make sense of the world do not relate merely to artefacts and nature but include their interactions with other people. Smiling, crying and cooing are not just mechanical responses to adult stimulation, but expressions that have the function of eliciting caring behaviour in return. Infants reach towards caregivers, and caregivers reciprocate by picking them up. Infants reach for something out of range, and caregivers reciprocate by handing them the object, which they receive with expressions of pleasure. These everyday interactions are, for the infant, an introduction to social life. Before long, young children begin to learn that they cannot get everything they want or do whatever they like. They may enjoy making a mess, only to experience their mother's irritation. They may take their siblings' toys and find them being snatched back again. They soon find out that their actions occur in a two-way street.

The point I wish to emphasise is that early moral experience grows out of the child's own explorations. This is not to deny that morality is a social affair, or that interactions with parents and other people help to shape the child's character and conduct. It is rather to remind us that the youngster's moral learning does not typically arise from instruction, but from the sum total of the responses of others to what they do. This way of learning is not unique to infancy, and continues throughout life. It is therefore something to consider when we think about moral education.

Moral education begins at home. By the time children enter school, their conduct and character have already been shaped by years of experience in the home environment. Some things have been allowed and others forbidden; some actions have been praised and others reprimanded. Parents and other caregivers in the home may have been permissive or strict, neglectful or attentive, abusive or temperate. Children have had to find ways of resolving conflicts with one another and of generally getting along with other people in their world. These things have already gone into the mix and will continue to do so.

Remember too that, before they begin school, many children will have spent a good deal of their waking lives in childcare and preschool. While such arrangements are in some regards an extension of the home, they bring young children into contact with an extended peer group as well as into a somewhat different relationship with adults. Mixing with other children throughout the day, in both structured activities and free play, provides constant opportunities for moral development in an environment that is likely to have a greater focus on social learning than will be the case at school. The relationship of childcare or preschool staff to children in their care is also more parental than that of teachers to students at school. Childcare and preschool form a bridge between the home and the school, and in no respect is this more so than when it comes to the business of socialisation.

Moral experience and the peer group

Even the most casual observation of the playground reveals that children are by no means a homogeneous social group. They tend to associate with others of their own age and to congregate in same-sex groups. Some children mix with a large range of individuals, whereas others are almost always to be found with close friends. Some boys and girls are popular and others are more socially isolated; some children are physically assertive and others are timid; some are constantly getting into scraps, while others shy away from conflict.

The community of peers in the playground reminds us that school-aged children's encounters with the moral domain are not entirely, or even primarily, ones that directly involve adults. Children are constantly evaluating conduct and character through their interactions with one another. They argue with each other about the rights and wrongs of actions. They defend or criticise the motives of third parties. They add emoticons to their text messages to signal their intentions. They call each other names, which are often criticisms of character. And anyone who has witnessed a debate between students as to whether the treatment meted out to them by a teacher is fair will know how heartfelt moral debate among children can be.

The community of peers is tempered by the presence of the teacher and educational demands when students move from the playground into the classroom. Even then, it remains a potent influence, and we should make productive use of it when it comes to the way that we teach moral education.

Differences of belief and opinion

As was argued in the introduction, it is not appropriate to run moral education in government schools on a religious basis. Even so, moral education cannot ignore the fact that the moral beliefs and outlook of a significant portion of students in government schools cannot be disentangled from their religion. It is therefore necessary to take this into account when devising a program of moral education.

It is obviously inappropriate for a government school program in moral education to contradict the teachings of the various faiths to which students may adhere. Nor can those teachings be left entirely out of account. To be educationally sound, the program must address the beliefs and understandings of students. One way of trying to address this issue is for moral education to stick to what everyone can agree to be common ground. When I say 'common ground', I am not just speaking of that which is common to the various faiths, of course, but of that which would be regarded as morally acceptable by the community as a whole.

It is possible to find general agreement on a basic set of moral principles and precepts so long as we do not subject them to critical examination. Let us take a simple example. Honesty is a value held by the community as a whole. (Some individuals pay scant regard to it, of course, but that is another matter.) But now, what does the value of honesty amount to and how is it to be justified? Does it mean that we should always tell the truth, for example, irrespective of the consequences? Some people think so, but others do not. Is there nothing wrong with a little white lie? If so, why is that—and if not, why not? In sticking to common ground, we might point out these disagreements, at a stretch, but we certainly should not try to consider who is right. What honesty requires and why it does so cannot really be considered. All that can be said is that some people believe one thing, while others believe something different; that some would give this reason, while others would give that one.

Teachers should be prepared to bring different views to the table and allow them to be considered. Such a process may be thought to undermine students' opinions, but the development of greater tolerance and mutual understanding is by far the greater effect. In fact, there's no greater reinforcer of our beliefs than examining their foundations and being able to justify them. Sometimes we do come to doubt our opinions, of course, but to do so because we see that they lack adequate justification is hardly a bad thing.

In saying that the alternative to eliding over differences of student belief and opinion is the examination of them, I am not advocating a debating contest involving set propositions that students have been asked to argue for or against. We are dealing with suppositions and beliefs that have an important place in the daily lives of students. Given this, we need thoughtful engagement across difference rather than an argumentative competition.

Moral education and our vision of society

Our approach to moral education cannot be separated from our vision of society. In order to see this, let us go back to the question of capacities. Is moral education to rely upon an appeal to reason, on the nurturing of sympathy, on strengthening of the will, or on something else? The nature of the capacities upon which morality depends has been a matter for discussion since ancient times. Thus, we find Plato beginning his dialogue called the *Meno* as follows:

> *Meno: Can you tell me, Socrates—is virtue something that can be taught? Or does it come by practice? Or is it neither teaching nor practice that gives it to a man but natural aptitude or something else? (1999, p. 354)*

Socrates replies that he knows nothing about virtue—not whether it can be taught, nor even what it is. While his profession of ignorance is something of a ruse designed to draw Meno into thinking about the nature of virtue, let us note that the three possibilities raised by Meno have different educational implications. Briefly, if virtue can be taught, then presumably it involves a body of knowledge or subject matter that a suitably trained teacher can impart. If it comes about simply through practice, then the teacher's role shifts from offering instruction to creating the opportunity for students to engage in virtue-building activities. And if virtue is inborn, it will express itself naturally. In that case, teachers should simply play their part in ensuring that moral growth does not become either warped through abuse or stunted by neglect.

We need to search around to discover Plato's views on this matter. At the conclusion of the *Meno*, he has Socrates tentatively suggest that virtue cannot be taught, but comes about through divine dispensation. For a more considered view, however, we may turn to the *Republic*, where Plato's response depends upon a distinction between two socially defined groups. There he tells us that proper knowledge and understanding of virtue is necessary for the rulers of society, while mere observance in practice is sufficient for everyone else. Those who rule must have genuine insight into true moral values, while the rest may take such matters on trust.

This social division implies two radically different schemes of moral education. In order to ensure that ordinary people conform to established notions of virtue, it is sufficient that they are brought up to have respect for them, to perceive things in those terms, and to become disposed to act accordingly through discipline and training. Being brought up to pledge allegiance to your country and to salute the flag as an exercise of patriotism is an example of this kind of training. As opposed to the moulding of feeling, action and character through discipline for the masses, the moral education reserved for Plato's ruling class is aimed at a direct apprehension or knowledge of 'the good' (see pp. 41–44). Such knowledge cannot be acquired by the former kind of training. Nor can it be handed down by a teacher as material to be learned. It must be sought through genuine inquiry, so that those who rule are able to uncover the truth about such matters for themselves. Correspondingly, their education must involve learning to think about moral matters, rather than simply being told what to think about them. In a word, their moral education must be *philosophical*.

It is still common enough for people to hold to Plato's view that, while society may need to educate a small class of individuals to think for themselves about moral matters, there is no benefit and perhaps considerable danger in treating everybody that way. But few people acquainted with the ideal society in Plato's *Republic* would these days fail to shudder at its totalitarian vision. It is a society in which the elite knowingly make use of the 'noble lie' in order to maintain social order over the general population. A guardian class defends the ideals worked out by the elite against both external and internal enemies. Strict censorship of writers and artists is enforced to ensure that the works they produce are in line with those ideals. Society decides on individuals' stations in life based on their capacity, and those positions are fixed. Private property is abolished among the ruling class, and women and children are held in common. According to Plato, this is all for the sake of the greater good.

Plato's utopian republic bears more than a passing resemblance to some twentieth-century totalitarian states, and should remind us of the inevitable ties that exist between moral education and the kind of society that we are trying to create. The creation of a society of philosopher kings, dispensing wisdom to the lower classes, requires a different scheme of moral education from one that aims to support democracy. It is a central theme of this book that collaborative ethical inquiry is the form that moral education should take if schools are to prepare children for life in a free and democratic society.

Those who take a conservative stance on moral matters may feel that morality is here being presented as something uncomfortably close to a tool of social engineering. It may appear to be disturbingly progressive, only adding to worries about where present attitudes to morality are leading us, when some would prefer to return to the values of the past. It cannot be denied, however, that societies are always on the move— technologically, economically and socially. Education must keep pace with these changes and help us to manage them. Moral education is as much an ingredient in the advancement of society as is scientific and technological education and we need to take a forward-looking approach to it.

It may be worth reminding ourselves that the lament over declining moral standards among the young is an age-old complaint. Rather than decrying the behaviour of the young or falling back on a sanitised version of the past, we would be better advised to fashion a moral vision of the future out of the possibilities of the present. This means working out how best to use the available ingredients to direct the course of social change.

Reference

Plato, *The collected dialogues*, eds E Hamilton & H Cairns, Princeton University Press, New Jersey, 1999.

CHAPTER 2

Educating for moral values

Personal responsibility, interpersonal relations, professional codes of conduct, political outlooks and educational policies all involve moral values. They shape the whole of the social domain that enfolds our life and being. In consequence, nothing could be of greater educational significance than attention to moral values.

While everyone accepts the importance of values education, the approach to be adopted in educating for values in the moral domain is a source of contention. Some follow Aristotle when he says in the *Nicomachean Ethics* that 'moral virtue comes about as a result of habit' (Book II) while others would agree with the great Swiss educational psychologist Jean Piaget (1999) that the child constructs his own moral world through interaction with peers. So should we be training students' moral habits or do we need to provide ample opportunity for students to construct their moral world through peer interaction? Should some other approach be tried? Just how are we to go about this crucial undertaking?

The traditional approach to moral education

Moral education has traditionally relied upon three elements: (1) moral instruction in the sense of telling or teaching students how they ought to behave; (2) use of rewards and punishments to regulate behaviour; and (3) character training through providing good models and wholesome experience.

Familiar as these approaches may be, they don't necessarily form a coherent set of strategies. Moral instruction is as ancient and yet familiar as Aesop's fables, and it is based on the presumption that morals can be taught. Character training, by contrast, adheres to the idea that moral values are things to be 'caught' rather than taught, as the old saying goes. They are something that we pick up by being exposed to them. If parents and teachers are fair in their dealings with children, then it is likely that the children in their care will be fair in their dealings with others. If parents and teachers are honest, then children will be honest; and so on. Coherent or not, it is this mixture of instruction with praise and reward, rebuke and punishment, good models and wholesome experience that form the basis of the traditional approach to moral education.

Let us briefly consider each of these elements in turn, beginning with moral instruction. On this way of proceeding, there are agreed moral values that are understood by the instructor and taught to the student. The values of fairness and honesty provide obvious examples. Fairness and honesty are socially approved values. Teachers presumably know what they involve, and their task in moral education is to find effective means of instructing students in them. The question is: Can we bring up young people to be fair and honest by instructing them to be so? If only things such as fairness and honesty were so unproblematic that, when faced with a relevant situation, any morally educated person would know what fairness or honesty demands. While there are cases where everyone would agree that what happened was grossly unfair or that someone was shamefully dishonest, there are many other cases where that is not so. Children are not the only ones to complain of what they take to be unfair treatment. While everyone can agree with the idea of 'a fair day's wages for a fair day's work', it is common enough for employees to feel hard done by even as employers take wages and conditions to be reasonable. Parties to an industrial dispute may express such views when trying to establish a bargaining position, of course, but they can also be the expression of genuine judgments clouded by self-interest. Even when industrial disputes are settled by independent arbitration, it is common for arbitrators to disagree among themselves. This only goes to show that balanced judgments as to what is fair are not always easily come by, and that while we can all subscribe to the motherhood statement that dealings should be fair, this does not get us very far in practice.

What is colloquially known as the 'carrot and stick' approach also has its drawbacks. Rewards and punishments may or may not prove effective in regulating behaviour, but they fail to supply adequate moral motivation and may actually help to undermine it. Students who act out of fear of punishment or from desire for reward are operating from prudential rather than moral motives. It is not just that they may behave otherwise if they figure that they will not get caught. From a moral point of view, we should be more concerned that someone motivated by rewards and punishments does not act from goodwill or out of concern for the consequences for others. Their motivation is self-centred. At its best, such an approach encourages what is known as ethical egoism. And while, at a stretch, ethical egoism can be regarded as a moral outlook, it is a very deficient one—as we will see in the next chapter.

Nor should we rely too heavily upon character training. We certainly should not pretend that in all the contingencies of life there is never really any doubt about what one ought to do, and that having the right kind of character will ensure that one does it. Being of what is conventionally called 'good character' will not prevent someone from acting out of ignorance, from being blind to the limitations of their own perspective, from being overly sure that they have right on their side, or even from committing atrocities in the name of such things as national security or faith. The parties to a conflict all too often take themselves to be upright in character and the obvious champions of good, while their antagonists are the personification of depravity and evil. History is littered with barbarities committed by men reputedly of good character who acted out of self-righteous and bigoted certainty. Far from being on solid moral ground, the ancient tradition that places emphasis on being made of the 'right stuff' has not prevented moral blindness towards those of different religion, ethnicity, skin colour, sexuality or politics—a blindness that has stymied reflective moral judgment and been responsible for a large portion of the preventable ills in human history.

I am certainly not denying that we should provide good models of things like fairness by engaging in fair dealings ourselves. I am suggesting, rather, that it is not enough. We also need to strengthen the capacity to factor and weigh relevant considerations in judging what is fair. This involves such things as having students learn to counter bias through looking at situations from other people's points of view, of forming the habit of scouting out facts rather than rushing to judgment, and of developing the ability to draw reasonable conclusions from the evidence.

Similar things can be said about other values to which we may subscribe. Let's go back to honesty. Of course we want students to be honest, and we cannot reasonably expect this unless we are honest in our dealings too. Still, we are not happy when a child is tactless. 'But it's the truth,' they assert. 'Yes, but you didn't have to say so.' Tact, as we know, is also a virtue, and we want children to learn to show respect for other people's feelings by tempering what they say. To some extent, children can learn to deal with the tensions that exist between truthfulness and tactfulness through good modelling by adults and the usual mixture of adult approval and correction of their conduct in this regard. A great deal more is to be gained, however, if children are given the opportunity to think about truthfulness and tact and their connection with all kinds of questions and issues in the moral domain. The distinction between lying and not necessarily inflicting what you think on others is important here, as is that between being deceitful and finding something more kindly to say. Even young children are perfectly capable of thinking about such things, and of being taught to raise and discuss related questions and issues. Here are some questions asked by members of a class of eight-year-olds who were discussing issues raised by reading a picture book of the classic story *The Boy Who Cried Wolf*:

- Is a lie being unfaithful?
- Can a lie be considered cheating somebody?
- Do you agree that a lie and a trick are the same?
- Are magicians liars?

It may astonish some people that young children can ask such questions and meaningfully discuss them, but it is no surprise to teachers who have been trained to engage students in collaborative philosophical inquiry. They realise that their students are capable of a far deeper understanding of such things than they are normally given credit for. They also know through experience that the careful consideration of such matters has implications for behaviour.

Without venturing further into the value of moral inquiry in the classroom, we should certainly question placing total reliance upon more traditional approaches to moral education. These need to be supplemented by moral inquiry. Only then will students be able to develop a really deep understanding of the concepts that reside in the moral domain and acquire the skills and abilities that underlie good moral judgment.

The social value of moral education

Before we go further in attempting to construct an alternative to traditional approaches to moral education, it will be helpful to think a little more about the relation between moral education and the wider vision of society raised in Chapter 1. Returning to the ancient world, we might recall that Socrates is reputed to have said that the unexamined life is not worth living. Famous though that saying is, it is a far cry from the conception of the 'good life' as we know it. We are familiar with concerns about social status, getting and spending, filling our spare time with entertainment or addiction to electronic gadgets, but not with thinking too deeply about our values. To the extent that we do so, we tend to regard it as a private rather than a public affair. This makes reflection a personal and inward journey rather than a social and collaborative one, and a person's values a matter of parental guidance in childhood and individual responsibility in maturity. The relegation of responsibility for moral values to the personal sphere also militates against societal self-examination. There is some public debate as to how we should live, yet it is very much the exception rather than the rule. Most examples of it that we find in the media appeal to a relatively narrow social stratum, leaving the rest of the field wide open to those traditional and self-styled custodians of values who profess to already have all the answers as to how we should live.

The relatively unreflective character of our society and the widespread presumption that values are a personal affair are symptoms of a chronic condition requiring remedy. It is something for which we need an educational prescription. The best way to prepare young people to enjoy life in a society that strives for the good in more than a material sense is by strengthening moral education in our schools. In order to create such a society we must educate for it.

Students need moral education to help them resist the ever-present appeal to narrow self-interest. They need it to enable them to find their way between the tyranny of unquestionable moral codes and the bankruptcy of individualistic moral relativism. They need it to help them engage productively across their differences rather than habitually responding to difference with suspicion or prejudice. On the larger scale and over the long term, our society needs it in order to sow the seeds of a less adversarial way of life in such things as politics, law, business and industrial relations. Selfishness, dogmatism, prejudice and mutual antagonism—such things are in plentiful supply in our society and we should not pretend otherwise. Yet rather than commiserate with one another as if there is nothing to be done, we can help to bring about improvement through moral education.

Not every approach to moral education is likely to achieve the benefits foreshadowed here. Broadly speaking, we need an approach that focuses less attention on teaching *that* and more on teaching *how*. We need one that emphasises collaboration and inquiry, rather than relying on individual learning and telling students what they should value. We need to teach students to develop good skills of judgment. And we need to include moral education throughout the curriculum, rather than regarding it as a stand-alone subject, or as something that can be taken care of by a school chaplain or in religious instruction. These are large and contentious issues. Let us take a closer look at them.

Teaching 'that' and teaching 'how'

Children are constantly being taught how to do things as well as being taught that things are thus and so, both in and out of school. When I was young I learnt my times tables by rote. I was taught *that* 2 × 2 = 4, *that* 3 × 2 = 6 and so on. I was taught many natural, historical and other kinds of facts, such as *that* whales are mammals and *that* the pyramids of Egypt were the burial places of the pharaohs. By contrast, however, I was also taught *how* to do things, such as *how* to tie up my shoelaces. This involved first watching my mother tie up my shoelaces and then having her assist me to tie them up.

Teaching *how* to do things normally involves some amount of teaching *that*. Teaching young children how to multiply by 2 involves teaching them such elementary facts as that 2 × 2 = 4 and that 3 × 2 = 6, just as teaching them how to tie up their shoelaces involves teaching them that they should first do this and then do that. However it isn't plausible to suppose that teaching people how to do things is just a matter of having them memorise facts or follow procedural instructions, except in artificial and circumscribed cases. While people may teach themselves to cook by following recipe books, for instance, someone who can prepare food only by following recipes has not learnt how to cook. Being able to cook is more than being able to follow a recipe book. Again, while some instruction is useful in teaching someone how to ride a bike, it is mostly a matter of having them try to ride. It is a case of learning by doing under guidance, and not of the teacher issuing a set of riding instructions that the learner subsequently carries out.

I emphasise the importance of teaching *how* because moral education cannot be reduced to issuing 'riding instructions'. Developing students' competence in making moral judgments involves teaching them how to use tools and procedures that have been found to be effective in making headway with moral matters—that is to say, by inquiring into them. Of course students cannot make headway without appropriate facts. If they don't know enough about the facts of a case, they can hardly be expected to make an appropriate moral judgment concerning it. Yet the development of good moral judgment involves more than knowing such facts. It involves using them to conjecture, explain, justify and reason about the moral worth of this, that and the other aspect of character and conduct.

This does not apply only to moral education, of course. It applies to teaching across the curriculum. Teaching students to engage in science is not the same thing as having them memorise scientific results. One can learn to repeat scientific facts and theories without gaining any real idea of how to engage in science. The same applies to the arts. It is one thing to teach students what others have said about a novel or to have them learn a poem by heart, and quite another to teach them how to critically evaluate what they read or how to make effective use of metaphor and simile. The point hardly needs to be made for areas such as physical education.

I do not deny that some things about the moral domain can be taught through teaching *that*. Students can be introduced to the teachings of great moral thinkers in this way, for example. But no amount of learning *that* can substitute for learning *how* to think in the moral domain.

Making inquiry collaborative

When I went to school, the old 'jug and mug' conception of pedagogy was still much in evidence. Simply put, it presumed the teacher to be knowledgeable and the students to be ignorant of the subject matter to be taught, with teaching involving its transfer from the teacher to the learner. That method of teaching involved one-way communication from the teacher to the student, and if the student communicated with anyone it was with the teacher. Talking to another student was likely to be regarded as a misdemeanour. When we move away from an emphasis on teaching *that* to teaching *how*, however, it is educationally desirable for students to engage with each other.

Let us see why this is so by considering a common feature of moral inquiry. When human conduct stimulates moral inquiry it is usually because that conduct is controversial, which is to say that there are different points of view as to how it should be judged. I may put forward one opinion while you offer another that does not look right to me. That gives both of us something to think about. If you and I have different opinions in regard to someone's conduct, then we are both in need of further justification and our views are subject to each other's objections. In fact, when we try to solve a moral problem of any complexity, we are often well-advised to discuss it with others.

This reliance upon others applies equally to the objectives of moral inquiry in the classroom. If we want students to grow out of the habit of going with their own first thoughts, to be on the lookout for better alternatives, and to become disposed to consider other people's points of view, then we cannot do better than having them learn by exploring moral issues, problems and ideas together. If we want them to become used to giving reasons for what they say, to expect the same of others and to make productive use of criticism, then we cannot go past giving them plenty of practice with their peers. And if we want them to grow up not to be so closed-minded as to think that those who disagree with them must be either ignorant or vicious, then the combination of intellectual and social engagement to be found in collaborative moral inquiry is just the thing. These are all good reasons for adopting this approach.

Educating for judgment

The American philosopher and educationalist John Dewey sets us off on the right track when it comes to thinking about the significance of educating for judgment in regard to values:

> *The formation of a cultivated and effectively operative good judgment or taste with respect to what is aesthetically admirable, intellectually acceptable and morally approvable is the supreme task set to human beings by the incidents of experience. (1980, p. 262)*

This makes the cultivation of judgment in regard to values the ultimate educational task and the development of good judgment central to moral education in particular. Indirectly, Dewey reminds us that moral education cannot be simply a matter of instructing students as to what they should value, as if they didn't need to inquire into moral values or learn to exercise their judgment. In any case, it is an intellectual mistake to think that moral values constitute a subject matter that can be learnt by heart. They are not that kind of thing. Moral values are embodied in commitments and actions and not merely in propositions that are verbally affirmed. Of course children need to learn about the shared moral values of their society—and about the moral values that are expressions of its cultural diversity, as well as about the moral values of people living in other times and places. But we cannot teach students to make good moral judgments merely by imparting such content.

This approach to moral education fits with the emphasis placed upon collaborative ethical inquiry for several reasons. First, the idea that moral values are to be cultivated by student reflection rather than impressed upon the student by moral authority from without supplies a way forward between an unquestioning attitude towards moral values and an individualism that makes each person their own moral authority. The development of good judgment through collaborative ethical inquiry is the path towards a truly social intelligence. Secondly, collaborative ethical inquiry depends upon different points of view. If something is uncontroversial and everyone is of the same opinion, then there is no motivation for inquiry. Inquiry arises in situations where something is uncertain, puzzling, contentious or in some way problematic. This is nowhere more in evidence than when students find that they have different opinions about some matter of moral value in the classroom. Through the attempt to resolve their differences they learn to inquire. Thirdly, collaborative inquiry is itself a kind of moral practice. Consider such elementary aspects of the practice as: learning to hear someone out when you disagree with what they are saying; learning to explore the source of your disagreement rather than engaging in personal attacks; developing the habit of giving reasons for what you say and expecting the same of others; being disposed to take other people's interests and concerns into account; generally becoming more communicative and inclusive. Such dispositions are those of a socially mature person and are surely among the outcomes to be attained if we are to help build a more morally intelligent society.

Moral education and the curriculum

It is possible to include collaborative moral inquiry in the curriculum as a stand-alone subject, but that is not wise. It gives the impression that moral concerns are something apart from the rest of the curriculum, as if such things as history and science are on a permanent moral holiday. Even if it did not do so, the separation would make it all but impossible for students to deal in any systematic way with the moral dimension of the subjects that they are studying.

Students need to learn to think about moral values in the various contexts in which questions about those values arise, and to deal with the moral dimension of each and every field of endeavour. Whether students are evaluating character in literature, considering conduct in history, thinking about our responsibility for the environment in science or working out what would be an equitable division in maths, they should be given the opportunity to bring their moral understanding to bear on each and every subject matter.

Teaching students how to make good moral judgments does not require the specialist training that teaching students to make artistic judgments or good decisions in a sport does. While ethical judgment requires skills that need to be taught, and any teacher who attempts to teach ethics needs to have an adequate knowledge of both the content and the skills involved, we are here primarily talking about applied ethics, which is the consideration of ethical issues and problems that arise in one or another subject matter, as in bioethics, environmental ethics, and so on. More specifically, we are talking about such issues as they arise within the subjects taught in school. In order to teach applied ethics in any subject, all you need is to know the subject and to have a basic knowledge of ethical theory and language. The introduction to these matters provided in Chapter 3 is sufficient to get you started.

Reconstructing ethics for educational purposes

Ethics is a branch of philosophy—a discipline sometimes seen as suitable only for tertiary study or for academically inclined students in the senior secondary years. Yet nothing could be more relevant to moral education than ethics. It is that branch of study in which we inquire into the moral domain, just as arithmetic is a branch of mathematics in which we inquire into the numerical domain. Although the work of professional ethicists tends to be abstract and technical, so that ethics may look to be too difficult to be included in anything but the senior school curriculum, the same is true of research in many of the disciplines that are represented in the standard curriculum from the earliest years of school.

Ethics has long been a popular area of study in upper secondary schools in other parts of the world, and in recent years philosophy has been making its way into the senior secondary curriculum in Australia. While this is a welcome development, it cannot be expected that interventions in the final years of school will have a really deep impact on the ways of thinking of the society or on the character of its concerns. Comparisons between the highly restricted place of ethics and the universal practice of exploring literature within the school curriculum may help to make the point. No one would expect a final-year survey course in literature to provide the kind of influence that growing up with literature imparts. From picture books in the early years to classics of English literature in the senior secondary school, we insist upon the study of literature, as well as engaging students in creative literary practice, throughout their education. We make such a thoroughgoing effort because we believe that it can have a formative influence. We believe that students can refine their sensibilities and develop a more humane cast of mind by growing up with literature, and learning to express themselves in speech and writing under its sway. In much the same way, for ethics to have a formative influence and thereby to significantly affect both the way people think and their moral values, it needs to be part of the regular fare throughout the school years. Only by this means can it effectively supply its nutrients to the developing roots of character and conduct.

In order to reconstruct ethics for these purposes, its subject matter needs to be adapted to the interests and experience of students of various ages and its tools and procedures adjusted to their stage of development. Ethics is no more difficult to recast in educational form than most other disciplines that have long since done so. Ethics is merely a late developer, educationally speaking.[1]

Having said this, I should point out that there is a view, going right back to Plato, that philosophical studies are suitable only for the academically gifted and mature scholar. Against this, it is worth recalling something that the educationalist Jerome Bruner asserted half a century ago. He made famous the claim that 'the foundations of any subject may be taught to anybody at any age in some form', and he suggested that the prevailing view of certain disciplines being too difficult for younger students results in us missing important educational opportunities (1960, p. 12). This is the conception that Bruner called a *spiral curriculum*: one that begins with the child's intuitive understanding of the fundamentals, and then returns to the same basic concepts, themes, issues and problems at increasingly elaborate and more abstract or formal levels over the years.

Whatever one may think of this conception in other areas of education, it is undoubtedly vital for developing the kind of understanding that belongs to ethics. Whether we are studying fairness, friendship or freedom, we return again and again to the same themes, the same basic concepts and issues. The theme of fairness in literature that is dealt with in a picture book in the first years of school may surface again in a story book for the young reader, to be taken up again in the adolescent novel and finally elaborated in much more complex and subtle ways in the major works of fiction that are on the syllabus in the senior secondary school. At each return, the student comes to the theme with more experience and more powerful ways of articulating that experience. And each return is an occasion for yet further development. Thus Bruner's claim about the foundations of the disciplines suggests that an early introduction to ethics is among the missed opportunities in education and alerts us to the possibility of introducing it to students from the first years of school.

---

1 See my *Sophia's question: thinking stories for Australian children* and accompanying *Teacher resource book* (2011) for a recent example of upper primary classroom materials for collaborative ethical inquiry.

Why not leave moral education to religious instruction?

Although we have already canvassed problems with a faith-based approach to moral education in government schools, they do make provision for religious instruction, and it seems reasonable to argue that this provides an appropriate venue for moral education for the great majority of students. In response, it is important to recognise that the moral dimension of religious instruction, while no doubt of value, cannot take on the burden that more properly falls to the regular school curriculum. Let us consider the matter.

To place moral education at the heart of what we do in schools, and to see it as continuous with all of our other efforts to educate the young, is to place it firmly in the curriculum rather than relegating it to religious instruction. Religious instruction is taught by instructors affiliated with the various faiths and denominations, and the content and methods of instruction are not integrated with either the school curriculum or its pedagogy. Religious instruction cannot take on the burden of a systematic exploration of the ethical issues involved in the various areas of the curriculum as they are presented throughout the rest of the week. It therefore cannot help but present morality in a somewhat disconnected fashion. And while it would be possible for religious instructors to adopt an inquiry-based approach to such matters, they are under no obligation to do so; many come from traditions that are likely to use the occasion to indoctrinate instead.

In schools that have an avowedly religious basis, religious instruction is likely to form an integral part of the education offered and to transmit the school's moral values accordingly. To the extent that the school honours the traditions of open discussion and critical reason (which can be found within all religions) it is likely that their moral education curriculum will be compatible with the approach being advocated here. After all, philosophy and religion have a long entangled history, and we should not think of them as incompatible when it comes to moral education in a religiously based school. The incompatibility is between the appeal to reason and dogmatism, wherever it may be found.

References

Aristotle, *The Nicomachean ethics*, book II, trans. WD Ross, available at <http://classics.mit.edu/Aristotle/nicomachaen.html>.

Bruner, J 1960, *The process of education*, Harvard University Press, Boston.

Cam, P 2011, *Sophia's question: thinking stories for Australian children*, Hale & Iremonger, Sydney.

Cam, P 2011, *Sophia's question: teacher resource book*, Hale & Iremonger, Sydney.

Dewey, J 1980 (1929), *The quest for certainty*, Perigee Books, New York.

Piaget, J 1999 (1932), *The moral judgment of the child*, Routledge, Abingdon.

CHAPTER 3

An introduction to ethics

What is ethics?

Ethics is the philosophical study of morality. It is concerned with the ends that we ought to choose and the considerations that should govern those choices, as well as with the kinds of people we should strive to be. Ethics is less interested in how people actually behave than with how they ought to behave. It seeks to understand the basis of moral obligation and the nature of 'the good'.

To inquire into the proper ends of human conduct is to seek to know what is good, just as to try to work out what kinds of considerations should govern our actions is to think about what makes an action right. Notice that to speak of 'good' and 'right' is to express moral matters in categorical or absolute terms; it is to treat morality as 'black and white'. It is therefore important to recognise that we also make comparative moral judgments. We allow that some motives or actions are better or worse than others, that some choices are morally more desirable than others, and that a person's conduct may have improved or declined. For younger students, we may couch the difference between absolute and comparative judgment by contrasting 'black and white' judgments with those that deal in 'shades of grey'. While some people are no doubt more inclined to see moral matters in absolute terms, and others tend to think comparatively, we all make use of both frameworks.

The emphasis being placed on moral judgment may suggest that the study of ethics teaches students to be judgmental. In order to avoid possible misapprehension, we need to note the distinction between being judgmental and exercising good judgment. To be judgmental is to be overly censorious of one's fellows, quick to disapprove of them and to persistently judge them ill. To exercise good judgment, by contrast, is to show discernment, perceptiveness and overall good sense. Exercising good judgment and being judgmental are therefore two very different things—so much so, that the development of good judgment helps us to avoid becoming judgmental.

A second misunderstanding to prevent at the outset is that when we use the word 'moral' we must be referring to conduct that is morally approvable. That is one use of the word. In that sense, 'moral' is the opposite of 'immoral'. To say that ethics is the philosophical study of the moral domain, however, is to use the word 'moral' in such a way that it contrasts with 'non-moral' rather than 'immoral'. This is generally how the word 'moral' is used in what follows. When we distinguish between moral and non-moral uses of words such as 'good' and 'right' we are engaged in elementary distinction-making of a kind that belongs to ethics.

There is no one correct way to lay out the subject matter of ethics. Although we began by taking it to deal primarily with conduct, some writers have emphasised character rather than conduct. Yet other writers have been more interested in analysing the nature of moral language than in dealing with moral issues and problems. Some have paid attention to the capacities required for being a moral agent, while others have been concerned with whether there can be bona fide moral agents in a world in which the laws of nature appear to rule out the possibility of free will. In addition to all this, various thinkers have defended different theories as to the nature of the good, developed different principles as guides to conduct and sought to justify those principles in a wide variety of ways.

This is to admit that ethics is not a cut and dried subject. We should not always expect agreement on even the most basic moral matters, nor expect ethics to provide settled answers to all kinds of ethical issues and problems. Since this is the outcome of some of the most thoroughgoing attempts to explore the moral domain, we should not pretend otherwise. We would do no service to students by presenting moral matters as entirely uncontroversial. That would be to encourage moral dogmatism, and to perpetuate the problems that so often attend moral controversy, when each party holds stubbornly to the conviction that those who disagree with them must be in the wrong. By contrast, to realise that there are different conceptions, principles and ways of looking at things is to begin to find your way around in the moral domain. It is to begin to be educated about such matters.

As no doubt you already appreciate, ethics is an extensive subject with a complex history. What follows therefore cannot hope to be anything other than introductory, and you will find suggestions for further reading at the back of the book.

The Good

We may talk about doing some good in the world, being of good character or living the good life. But what makes conduct, character or a life *good*?

In order to be clear about what we mean when we talk about the good, we need to make a distinction between the goodness of ends and the goodness of means to those ends. Some things are good for other things, but some, we might say, are good in themselves. Taking on more responsibilities at work may be a good way to advance your career, for instance, and all sorts of good may come of it, such as gaining a promotion and increasing your income, all of which may provide you with a greater sense of satisfaction and overall happiness. Hard work that leads to success in your career is by no means the only path to happiness, but it is a way of achieving satisfaction for many. It is good as a means. Happiness itself, by contrast, does not appear to be a means to anything further. It would be odd to ask what happiness is good for. Unlike taking on responsibilities or increasing your income, happiness is not good for attaining something else. It is, or has commonly been held to be, an end in itself—something inherently or intrinsically good.

Happiness is not the only thing that has been put forward as the end to attain. Other things have been taken to be inherently good, including pleasure, virtue, knowledge, beauty, friendship and adherence to duty. Some moral philosophers have held that, among all such things, there is just one ultimate end. It is arguable that Socrates thought of happiness as the greatest good, for example, and that even what he acknowledged to be virtues are good only in that they contribute to happiness. Other philosophers have acknowledged a plurality of ends, holding that there is no one thing to which all others are ultimately only a means, or to which they are reducible. Such a view allows that various goods are good in different ways, and admits the possibility that there can be genuine conflicts over what ends to pursue when a variety of choices suggest themselves as independently and inherently good.

Happiness has been the main contender for the greatest good, although there have been quite different conceptions of it. People often think of happiness as a feeling akin to pleasure, and that is certainly how it was understood by the English philosopher and social reformer Jeremy Bentham, whose account of the good equates it with happiness (Bentham 2007). For Bentham, it all comes down to maximising pleasure and minimising pain. By contrast, although Aristotle also thought of happiness as the only thing that we desire for its own sake, he interpreted it as a state of human flourishing through which our virtues are developed in accord with reason. On his account, happiness is a matter of 'doing well' rather than merely of 'feeling well'.

Although it is not my intention to attempt to adjudicate between such diverse views, you might like to consider the following thought experiment put forward by the contemporary American philosopher Robert Nozick. He asks us to imagine that advances in neuroscience have led to the construction of an 'experience machine' that can provide anyone who agrees to be connected to it with a simulated reality in which they experience a life full of pleasure. If pleasure were the only good, Nozick suggests, then we would have all the reason we need to plug into the machine (1974, pp. 42–45). We would be out of contact with reality, of course, and so wouldn't actually be doing the things that seem to bring us pleasure. Now, would you like to become permanently plugged into the experience machine? Nozick is betting that you would not.

Not all philosophers have been satisfied with the idea that the good can be specified in terms of fixed ends such as the achievement of happiness. John Dewey (1957) argued that nothing can be prescribed as good for all people in every circumstance of life, and that there is no such thing as *the* good life any more than there is such a thing as *the* good dinner. Many different meals may make good dinners, depending upon such things as one's culinary tastes and dietary requirements, time constraints and the time of year. Similarly, what is morally good in one context might not be so in another; and what is genuinely a good for some people may not be good for everyone. The good depends upon the circumstances, according to Dewey, and consequently needs to be discovered by inquiring into them.

Someone who rejects fixed ideals and ends is more likely to see moral life as a continuing process of 'better' and 'worse' rather than one of seeking 'the good' as a supreme and final achievement. Here again is Dewey:

> *Not perfection as a final goal, but the ever-enduring process of perfecting, maturing, refining is the aim in living. Honesty, industry, temperance, justice ... are not goods to be possessed as they would be if they expressed fixed ends to be attained. They are directions of change in the quality of experience. Growth itself is the only moral 'end'. (p. 177)*

Alongside their connection with moral improvement and decline, 'better' and 'worse' are associated with alternatives between which a choice is to be made. All too often, people go on to choose the worse over the better—

not knowingly, of course, but out of ignorance, misunderstanding or lack of foresight. To the extent that moral choices are like forks in the road, we are reminded of the need for good judgment—and of the educational imperative to develop it.

Philosophers have differed over where to place the good in their accounts of morality. Some have put it first, and then characterised right action in terms of promoting the good. If the good is regarded as maximising human happiness, for instance, then the right thing to do is to act so as to promote that end. This was Bentham's view, as we saw. Other accounts put moral principles ahead of the consequences of action, and see the good as residing in the subjection of our will to them. Right action is then action in conformity to those principles. If keeping your promises is an inviolable principle, for example, then it would be right to keep them, come what may. The 18th-century German philosopher Immanuel Kant argued along these lines, claiming that we have an absolute moral duty to keep our promises. Yet other accounts focus upon morally commendable character traits, rather than on conduct, and see the good as flowing from them. Aristotle took this approach. Later we will look more closely at all three kinds of accounts, but for now let us turn our attention to the topic of right action.

Right action

There are basically two schools of thought about the proper basis of moral decision-making. According to one, actions are morally justified insofar as their consequences promote the good, be that pleasure, happiness or whatever. The other school has it that actions are to be justified by reference to moral rules, principles or duties, rather than to consequences. The difference is easy to see if we go back to Kant's claim that we have an absolute duty to keep our promises. From this it follows that keeping one's promise is always the right thing to do. Of course, keeping a promise may sometimes have undesirable consequences, even readily foreseeable ones, and if we were to judge actions by their consequences, then we might not be justified in keeping a promise in such circumstances. Indeed, we may be right to break it. Just suppose that you promised to spend the evening with friends, but late in the day a pile of work lands on your desk and it is imperative that it is done right away. Otherwise, as we say, there will be consequences. If you should always keep your promises, then you should go out with your friends. If the consequences are to be your guide, then you should probably get on with your work and trust that your friends will understand. In any event, the two approaches to moral decision-making may deliver contrary outcomes.

To claim that actions are to be justified by their consequences places an onus on us not just to look ahead, but, on many occasions, to investigate the possible consequences of choosing between various options that are open to us. This may be a challenging requirement. Suppose that we were to take pleasure as a basis for our estimations. Then we would need to be able to make at least a reasonable estimate of how much pleasure is likely to accrue from one course of action as opposed to another in order to know what we should do. Not all pleasures are going to be of equal worth, of course, and so we would need to take that into account. To be consistent in our approach, estimating the worth of a given pleasure may require us to work out the longer-term consequences of pursuing one kind of pleasure rather than another. Details aside, it is obvious that this approach to moral decision-making is heavily reliant upon our knowledge of the likely consequences of our conduct, both immediately and in the long run. In placing a premium on the acquisition and application of such knowledge, this approach to moral judgment can be characterised as empirical and deliberative.

I began by saying that this approach contrasts with one that treats moral decisions as a matter of principle. Yet those who are minded to look to the consequences can formulate principles too. 'Always act so as to promote the greatest possible balance of pleasure over pain' is a moral principle that refers us to the consequences of action. So it might be more accurate to say that those who take the opposing view are not willing to base moral principles on the consequences of acting upon them. They attempt to justify them in other ways.

How else might moral principles be justified? Well, they might be taken to issue from some authority, and traditionally the appeal has been to divine authority. Those who make such an appeal would say that if God commands us to act (or to refrain from acting) in various ways, then we ought to unquestionably obey. Right action is action consistent with the will or commandments of God. This is known as the Divine Command Theory of morality. As with the other justifications to be mentioned below, it is not my intention to engage in any lengthy debate as to the merits of such a view. Suffice it to say that the classical argument against it goes right back to Plato. Let us ask: Is an action right because God commands us to behave in that way, or does God command us to do so because it is right? If an action is right because God commands it, then no matter what God commanded us to do, it would be right simply because he commanded it. Were God to command us to commit murder, then it would be right. (Someone might say that God would never command us to do such a thing. Perhaps so, but that's not relevant. It only matters that *were* he to do so, then it be would become right.) The alternative, of course, is that God commands us to do things because they are right. While not open to the same challenge, this implies that the standards of right action don't depend on them being commanded by God. Contrary to the theory, God's commandments themselves depend upon the standards of right action.

It is sometimes thought that the principles of morality are self-evident and in need of no further justification. In its most common version, this is the notion that anyone who is not deranged or corrupt can intuitively tell right from wrong. Such a view may at first seem plausible, but it does not stand up to the evidence. Plato and Aristotle were neither corrupt nor deranged, and both were deeply interested in the moral life and contributed much to our understanding of it. Yet neither of them saw anything wrong with slavery. Ancient Athenian society, so often admired as the cradle of democracy, was built upon slave labour. This was a familiar and accepted fact of life that even its philosophers did not question. If the principles of morality were self-evident, so that anyone who had not lost their moral compass could intuitively tell right from wrong, how then could Plato and Aristotle not have been struck by the fact that slavery is wrong? To take an example much closer to home, while abortion is not the heated social issue that it was some years ago, there are still many people in our own society who believe it to be wrong. If it is wrong, then, on the present view, that fact is self-evident. Yet whatever the rights and wrongs of the issue may be, it can hardly be said that those who first presented the case for abortion were arguing in the face of something that everyone immediately knew to be wrong. We could multiply examples by the dozen to show that the claim to the intuitive self-evidence of moral principles does not stand scrutiny.

Even if the claim to intuitive self-evidence cannot be sustained, it may be that the central claims of morality stand to reason. That is to say, while we may not be able to argue that they are self-evident to unaided intuition, we may be able to show that they become self-evident when seen in the clear light of reason. Immanuel Kant is most famous for this line of thought, and we may begin to get a grip on what he has to say by returning to the example of promise-keeping. Can we show by appeal to reason that we ought to keep our promises? Suppose that it suits us to break a promise. Is that acceptable, in principle? Well, we can't consistently excuse ourselves without allowing that others may do so when it suits them. Yet that would mean we could never rely on people to keep their promises. Although people might say that they promise to do something, it wouldn't amount to more than saying that they will do so if it suits them. In other words, the proposal to break our promise cannot consistently be put into practice. Kant argued that all of our major moral precepts can be established by a similar kind of appeal to reason, as we will see later in more detail.

Normative ethical theories

Now let us take a closer look at the three kinds of approaches to moral judgment identified above: those that look to the consequences of an action in order to judge it; those that rely upon rules and principles in order to determine the rightness of an action independently of its consequences; and those that take character, rather than action, to be the primary object of moral concern. These three methods are sometimes referred to as *normative* ethical theories, because they deal with moral standards or *norms* by which to regulate conduct or appraise character.

Teleological theories

Moral theories that view ends as justifying actions are said to be *teleological*. [1] In order to gain more insight into the nature of such theories, let us return to Jeremy Bentham, who propounded the famous modern teleological theory known as *utilitarianism*.

According to Bentham, as we saw earlier, the sole good for which people ultimately strive is the experience of pleasure and avoidance of pain. As it stands, this claim is ambiguous. Is it being said that people equate the good with their own pleasure or is it meant to include the pleasure for others as well? Obviously, people who constantly seek their own pleasure, irrespective of the consequences for others, should be distinguished from those who do not. Such is the goal of the *ethical egoist*. This is not because the ethical egoist is necessarily selfish or egotistical. An ethical egoist believes that everyone should try to maximise their own satisfaction. It is a moral theory rather than a psychological condition—which is not to say that it is justifiable. Indeed, ethical egoists face difficulties in seeking to maximise their own pleasure while holding that everyone should do likewise. It seems certain that were others to follow the egoist's policy, it would sometimes detract from the pleasure of the egoist. What is to the benefit of others may also be of benefit to the egoist on occasion, but surely not all of the time.

---

1   *Telos* is classical Greek for 'end'.

This means that an ethical egoist's advice cannot consistently be given to others. In those cases where asserting that others should try to maximise their own pleasure is likely to lead to a loss of pleasure for the egoist, the egoist is not acting consistently with the moral dictum that people should always seek to maximise their own pleasure.

Whatever one thinks of ethical egoism, it needs to be distinguished from a moral stance like Bentham's which requires us to try to maximise pleasure and minimise pain across the board. Unlike egoism, this may demand self-sacrifice. We may need to rein in our own gratification in order to produce the best outcome overall. As difficult as it may be for some of us to follow such a policy, there is nothing self-contradictory about it. In at least a fair proportion of cases, however, there are going to be other problems in attempting to maximise what Bentham calls *utility*. For one thing, we need to be able to estimate the sum total of pleasure (or trade-off between pleasure and pain), and it may be difficult if not impossible to do so reliably. Our actions may have unforeseen consequences, for example, and it is far from obvious that we can rate all pleasures on a single scale so as to quantify them and calculate their sum. Aside from these difficulties, the press of circumstances may require a rapid response, with little time available to arrive at the kind of estimate that the policy requires.

At least part of the difficulty may be solved by drawing up some rules for guidance, instead of having to engage in busywork for each individual act. This is the difference between what is called *act utilitarianism* and *rule utilitarianism*. Rule utilitarians need not try to work out what to do every time from scratch—every time they *act*—but rely instead upon *rules* that have been proven to maximise utility. Thus, a rule utilitarian may agree with Kant that we should obey the rule to keep our promises. This is not because we can prove that we should always keep our promises simply by an appeal to reason. It isn't because doing so will maximise pleasure or minimise pain on each and every occasion—which obviously it won't. Rather, it's because we will be able to maximise utility overall and in the long run by obeying the rule. Alternatively, the rule utilitarian might treat moral rules as rules of thumb, rather than ones that apply without exception. That is to say, the rule utilitarian might argue that we can maximise the outcome by *normally* following the rule, while overriding it on those occasions when following it is clearly outweighed by the potential for harm.

The problem of trying to adjudicate between different kinds of pleasures was not lost on Bentham's successor, John Stuart Mill, who famously remarked: 'It is better to be a human being dissatisfied than a pig satisfied; better to be Socrates dissatisfied than a fool satisfied.' He went on to say: 'And if the fool or the pig is of a different opinion, it is because they only know their own side of the question. The other party to the comparison knows both sides' (2008, p. 140). In other words, while one kind of pleasure may be more worthwhile than another, the person who has known both will have no difficulty judging which is the 'higher' and which is the 'lower' pleasure, as Mill calls them. Unfortunately, this does not solve the utilitarian's problem of factoring in various kinds of pleasures in order to maximise the outcome. Ordering pleasures is one thing and quantifying them is another. And it isn't obvious that such different enjoyments as those of the theme park and the concert hall can be converted into common coin.

What many would consider to be a far more devastating criticism of utilitarianism arises from the fact that it appears to allow for outcomes that are shockingly unfair. Bentham employed the moral principle of always acting so as to promote the greatest happiness of the greatest number to give expression to the idea that public policy should always consider everyone's welfare, and not afford privilege to the few while neglecting the disadvantaged and the poor. Yet the utilitarian principle appears to offer no safeguard against causing pain to some person, or group of people, if that promotes the best outcome in terms of the overall balance of pleasure over pain. This includes sacrifice or torture of the innocent, otherwise arbitrary dispossession, arrest or imprisonment, and any number of what we would ordinarily regard as injustices. On utilitarian grounds, it seems that such things would be right so long as they contribute to the greater good. It may well be that these unwanted possibilities can be ruled out by other means. We can legislate against them, for example. Yet making them illegal is of little help to the utilitarian. Nearly everyone would regard these things as immoral and it is far from clear that they are ruled out on moral grounds by the greatest happiness principle.

Finally, it is not enough for people to desire pleasure. The utilitarian needs to show that the pleasures we desire are desirable. There is a difference, after all, between the desired and the desirable, the wanted and the worthwhile, and only the latter is morally approvable. Mill's response to this problem is simply to assert that the fact people desire something is the only proof available or needed to show it is desirable. 'The only proof capable of being given that an object is visible is that people actually see it', says Mill; and in the same way, 'The sole evidence it is possible to produce that anything is desirable, is that people do actually desire it' (p. 168). This is a desperate remedy if ever there was one. People can desire and take pleasure in all manner of things of which virtually no one would morally approve. We need to evaluate our pleasures and enjoyments rather than aiming to experience as much pleasure as possible, regardless of its basis or of the things that might flow from it. Even so, the defect points to the cure. The obvious thing to do is to inquire into the sources and consequences of the pleasures that we seek. Some of the things in which we take pleasure confer additional benefits, while others are idle. Some pleasures are innocent, while others prove harmful—and they may be harmless on one occasion but not on another. It is only on the basis of further assessment on a case-by-case basis that their true moral worth can be known.

The fact that pleasures cannot be taken at face value shows that things are more complicated than simply following rules that are thought to confer the greatest overall happiness. Instead, we need to consider pleasure as a value that is under trial. We may value this or that pleasure, but should we do so? Much depends upon its causes and consequences. If the pleasure were the result of being plugged into Nozick's experience machine (or, to take a real life example, habitually injecting a mind-altering substance) it would have a different value than if it were the result of accomplishment brought about by our efforts. Again, if the pleasure we take in something spurs us on to further attainment, then it is arguably of more value than a passing enjoyment that bears no fruit. In short, the causes and consequences of our pleasures are matters for investigation and the value we place upon them may be adjusted accordingly.

The idea that pleasures are warranted by the evidence, rather than being the unexamined end of all right action, leads to a philosophical outlook known as *pragmatism*. According to the pragmatist, the causes and consequences of seeking pleasure (or any other value) on a given occasion provide a test of its merits. This is a kind of successor to utilitarianism that we met with in the philosopher John Dewey when he said that goods are not fixed ends, and that each case needs to be decided by an examination of the particular circumstances that attend it: that one course of action may be better than another depending upon a comparison of the consequences that each may have for the quality of experience and moral growth of those involved.

None of this proves that we should decide what to do by looking to the consequences, of course. In order to see how else we might determine what we should do, let us turn to deontological moral theories.

Deontological theories

Deontological theories deny that the morally right thing to do is determined by non-moral goods such as pleasure or happiness that are likely to result. Rather, on the deontological model, independently established moral laws, principles or duties tell us how we should conduct ourselves. As we saw, the Divine Command Theory says that an action is right because it conforms to the will of God. Even if we stand to benefit from our acting in this way, our actions are not made right by the rewards that we may derive. Similarly, those who hold that it is our moral duty to act in accord with our intuitions claim that we can tell immediately whether an action is right without investigating the consequences. Such accounts are deontological.[2]

As with teleological theories, there are both *act-deontologists* and *rule-deontologists*. Those who would have us do what our moral intuitions dictate are likely to be act-deontologists. When faced with a particular situation, they believe that we need only consult our intuitions about that case in order to know whether a proposed course of action is right or wrong. This is different from following moral rules such as the Golden Rule or the Ten Commandments. A person who judges right from wrong by referring to such rules is a rule-deontologist.

We criticised implicit reliance upon our moral intuitions in our discussion of right action, and may set that aside for now. It will be sufficient for our purposes to return to Kant, who provides us with what is probably the most famous rule-based deontological theory (1964). Let us begin with Kant's interpretation of the good. If we were to ask ourselves what is the greatest or highest good, says Kant, it cannot be something that is good only occasionally—something good in some circumstances but not in others. Therefore, the good cannot be found in our intellectual capacities, because they can be used for evil purposes as well as for good, depending upon our resolve. Nor can the good be found in our temperament or character. Even such qualities as loyalty and courage can support unspeakable acts in the name of some cause. The same is even more obviously true of worldly power and fortune. Not even happiness is unconditionally good. It may be undeserved or derived from things that are otherwise objectionable. The one thing good in all circumstances, says Kant, is a good will. It cannot be turned to immoral purposes while remaining good. A good will is unconditionally good. This does not mean that a good will is good because of its accomplishments, which often depend upon circumstances beyond a person's control. A good will is good in itself.

---

2   A term based on the Greek 'deon', meaning duty or obligation.

What is it to act from good will? According to Kant, it is to act out of respect for the moral law—not merely to conform to it through habit or convention, nor to do so in the hope of attaining some benefit. It is to behave in that way because you see it as your duty. But now, if the greatest good is to see it as your duty to respect the moral law, we need to know what the moral law prescribes. Kant spells this out in more than one way, but we will consider only his first formulation for the sake of brevity: 'Act only on that maxim through which you can at the same time will that it should become a universal law' (1964, p. 39). By a maxim, Kant means a rule of conduct that we intend to act upon, whether or not we ought to do so. In order to determine whether we can act upon such a maxim with good will, we need only ask ourselves whether we would want everyone to behave in that way. Here is Kant:

> *I need no far-reaching ingenuity to find out what I have to do in order to possess a good will. Inexperienced in the course of world affairs and incapable of being prepared for all the chances that happen in it, I ask myself only, 'Can you also will that your maxim should become a universal law?' (p. 71)*

In order to see how Kant's proposal is meant to work, let us consider an example or two. Suppose that a man is in need of money. While he could ask for a loan, he knows that he would not be able to pay it back. Even so, we can imagine him acting on the maxim that when he is short of money, he should be free to borrow it on the false promise of paying it back. Now let us test this maxim against Kant's principle. Can the man will that everyone should act according to this maxim? Well, if everyone were to do what he proposes, then no one would lend money to anyone who needed it. They would know full well that the promise of repayment was a sham. Therefore, Kant concludes that the maxim cannot consistently be adopted. It is self-defeating. While we would lose the benefit of obtaining loans were it possible for this kind of false promising to become universal, it is important to note that this isn't Kant's point. Rather, he is saying that the practice couldn't become universal because it would be destroyed along the way. It follows from this that the maxim cannot be put into practice consistent with his moral law. By contrast, of course, we can will it to be a universal maxim that people should keep their promises to do what they can to pay back money they owe. There's no contradiction in that.

To take a second example, Kant considers a well-to-do man who feels no need to offer support to others who are struggling, even though he could easily help them. The man's maxim is that he need not do anything to relieve the distress of those in need. In this example there is no contradiction in supposing that everyone could adopt this maxim. It may not be desirable, but it is possible. Yet can the prosperous man consistently *will* it to be so? Kant argues that he cannot, because that would involve willing that he should receive no support from others come the day that he is in need of support himself. Hence he cannot universalise his maxim, and so cannot act upon it with good will. There is no such difficulty in acting upon the contrary maxim that we should assist those in need when we are able. This makes it clear where our moral duty lies.

Kant's notion that any rational individual can readily determine the moral commands to which we should all adhere may appear naïve when we consider the fact that debate and disagreement is a pervasive feature of the moral domain. Still, Kant supposes himself to have provided us with a means of settling such disputes, and so we need to see how it fares.

As it turns out, it has its share of problems. For one thing, conflicts can occur between our various Kantian duties. Take the two mentioned above. Circumstances may arise where keeping a promise to repay a debt would prevent a person from helping someone in need. This suggests that our duties are not as absolute as Kant takes them to be. Of course, we could write provisos into our maxims to try to cover all such cases, but there is a real danger in attempting to do so. It looks as though we will end up with rules so hedged about that they apply only in specific circumstances. In effect, we may well be forced into reverting to act-deontology.

One might also wonder whether Kant is right in what he says about examples. Take the case of the wealthy man. Might not someone who is self-sufficient, and in no real danger of falling into poverty, accept the risks involved in everyone adopting his policy? There seems to be no contradiction in his doing so. In that case, however, he can consistently will his maxim to be adopted by everyone. While a single failure of this kind may not wholly undermine Kant's case, it is clearly more difficult to prosecute than he imagines.

Finally, it is entirely possible to adopt a policy of assisting others in need because (to follow Kant's own line of thought) you never know when you may be in need of help yourself. Yet if that were your *motivation* for helping others, then your actions would be self-serving rather than being driven by recognition of your moral duty. In other words, you could adopt a policy of helping others, and desire that they do likewise, purely out of self-interest rather than from good will. Therefore Kant's requirement that we must be willing for everyone to adopt our policies may be a necessary condition for them to be morally acceptable, but it doesn't seem to be something we can solely rely upon.

The objections raised to Kant's account do not rule out the claim that it takes us down the right track, nor do they prove that a deontological approach to ethics is mistaken. They do show, however, that knowing whether an action is right is not as straightforward as answering Kant's question as to whether we can consistently will that others should follow suit.

Virtue ethics

So far, we have been considering approaches to ethics that look to consequences, or to rules and so forth, in order to guide and evaluate conduct. Yet, in everyday life, we are as likely to admire or deplore aspects of a person's character as to judge their behaviour. Even when we praise or condemn what someone does, we often take this to reflect upon the kind of person they are—whether they are honest or deceitful, trustworthy or unreliable, good natured or cantankerous, and so on. Traits like honesty and reliability are virtues in a person, and what is known as *virtue ethics* places emphasis upon such things, rather than seeing moral evaluation as having to do primarily with the consequences of actions or their conformity to rules.

Such a view prevailed in classical antiquity, and it exercised a strong influence on Western moral philosophy right up to the beginning of the modern period, when it was largely displaced by Kantian moral theory and then utilitarianism, in turn. Interest in virtue ethics has re-emerged in recent years, however, becoming a field of study in its own right as well as encouraging the other two approaches to moral theory to also pay attention to character and not just to conduct.

From Aristotle's first classifications of them, the virtues were connected with happiness, in the sense in which that is equated with wellbeing and fulfilment. This is not to think of happiness as a feeling such as pleasure. We may take pleasure in things that make us happy, but we cannot equate happiness with pleasure. For pleasure may or may not be life-enhancing, depending upon what we take pleasure in. It is rather to conceive of it as the condition that parents wish for when they want their children to be happy in life. On the view that we are presently considering, that kind of life is achieved by cultivating the virtues. As Aristotle expresses it in the *Nichomachean Ethics*, 'happiness is an activity of the soul in accordance with perfect virtue' (Book I).

Since Aristotle has been the most influential source of this approach to ethics, let us look a little further at how he proceeds in order to get a deeper understanding of it. The idea that the virtues are to be cultivated implies that they are not purely natural capacities, but are at least in part a product of education or training. In fact, Aristotle conceives of them as habits that begin to be established by being brought up to behave in certain ways. Many small acts of courage help to make you courageous—they build your capacity to be courageous when, later on, greater challenges present themselves. By engaging in everyday acts of fair exchange you learn to be just. Through being brought up to consider the views of others you learn to be considerate, and so on.

It is important not to confuse habit with impulse. If an action is purely impulsive, then it cannot be virtuous. Good moral habits require discernment. Consider actions that call for courage. An experienced mountaineer is all too well aware of the foolhardiness of an act that appears but a bit of derring-do to a novice. A highwire act may look virtually suicidal to someone who lacks the performer's skill and judgment. Although the consideration of courage in such cases may not seem to us a moral one, it does point to a relationship between virtue and judgment. Practically speaking, moral choice requires us to make judgments regarding possible actions or responses, and virtue lies in choosing well.

According to Aristotle, the kind of discernment required here is that which leads to a proportionate response. We can see what that means by considering what he says about courage. As he conceives it, courage lies between rashness, on the one hand, and cowardice, on the other. It represents the 'Golden Mean' between the two. If we know that something is much to be feared and yet someone responds dismissively, we see that as recklessness. If something is relatively harmless, by contrast, and they behave as if it were the most fearful thing, then we will regard that as lily-livered. In short, the excessively fearful person behaves in a cowardly fashion, while the insufficiently fearful one behaves rashly. In either case, poor judgment leads to a disproportionate response.

Aristotle says the same kind of thing about all of the moral virtues that he considers, whether concerned with self-restraint, money matters, honour, temper or social intercourse. To be temperate is to incline neither to self-denial nor to self-indulgence. It is a virtue with money to be neither a miser nor a spendthrift. To take due pride in what you do is to slide neither into vanity nor into self-effacement. The good-tempered person is neither irascible nor overly amenable. Friendliness inclines to candour and descends into neither flattery nor insult. And to have a ready wit is to be neither a buffoon nor humourless. In all such cases, we may picture virtue as standing at the balancing point between a pair of vices that lie at opposite ends of the spectrum.

Critics have complained that the virtues cannot always be conceived of in this way. The British philosopher Bertrand Russell is one who took this view.

> *Some virtues do not seem to fit into this scheme; for instance, truthfulness. Aristotle says that this is a mean between boastfulness and mock-modesty, but this only applies to truthfulness about oneself. I do not see how truthfulness in any wider sense can be fitted into the scheme. There once was a mayor who had adopted Aristotle's doctrine; at the end of his term of office he made a speech saying that he had endeavoured to steer the narrow line between partiality on the one hand and impartiality on the other. The view of truthfulness as a mean seems scarcely less absurd. (1961, p. 186)*

It is definitely a virtue in someone to be honest, and not merely in the way that they present themselves. And it would indeed be silly to say that honesty lies in the middle between being completely truthful and being a total liar, by analogy with Russell's mayor. But maybe we can extend Aristotle's idea. Maybe to be honest is, more generally, neither to exaggerate something nor to downplay it. An honest person is someone who tells it like it is.

Even if Aristotle's scheme can be made to work right across the range of virtues, there are other problems. Let us confine ourselves to what is probably the most important of them. Aristotle presents us with a range of virtues that upper-class Athenians would have found no reason to question. It may be why he provides no justification for his list. This would be less of a problem if the same dispositions were regarded as virtues at all times and in all places. But that simply isn't so. Aristotle's own pinnacle of moral virtue, the magnanimous man, comes across as a vain and condescending aristocrat to modern sensibility. To take a more extreme example, well-known to Aristotle, consider the moral outlook of the heroic age depicted in Homer. This is literature, of course, but it is still a portrayal that resonates with the ancient world. The contrast is well summed up by Will Durant:

> *The good man is not one that is gentle and forbearing, faithful and sober, industrious and honest; he is simply one who fights bravely and well. A bad man is not one that drinks too much, lies, murders, and betrays; he is one that is cowardly, stupid, or weak. (1939, p. 50)*

Those who, like Aristotle, accentuate the importance of character are inclined to acquiesce with the accepted virtues of their day. In taking them as given, they dismiss without argument any challenge to their values. Yet, to insist on unquestioning acceptance of ancient upper-class Athenian virtues—or, for that matter, the values of middle-class contemporary Australians—is unsustainable. It is illicitly to infer what ought to be from what is. It is to imply that if we think something is good or right, then it is good or right, no matter what others may think or have thought. Of course, we can always say that while our values may not be absolutely and unquestionably right, they are right *for us*. But we need to note that this is to accept a form of cultural relativism.

In looking briefly at Aristotle's ethics, I have said nothing about the close connection that he sees between ethics and politics, or introduced you to what he says about the intellectual as opposed to the moral virtues. In the end, Aristotle claims that the most excellent sort of life for a human being is the life of the mind, because it allows us to most fully exercise our distinctive capacity for reason. But then, what else would you expect from a philosopher?

* * *

As we have seen, moral theories have traditionally taken three forms. Teleological theories begin with some end that they take to be good and then identify right action as directed to that end. Deontological theories seek to establish right action through moral duties, principles or laws, irrespective of the consequences. Virtue theories start with traits that define the good in someone, and then see right action in terms of the ways in which someone with such traits would conduct themselves.

Even from the little that has been said, it is clear that each approach has its strengths as well as its problems. In extreme cases, it is easy to see their weaknesses. We would all condemn someone who knowingly ordered the torture of innocent people for the greater pleasure of others. Only a zealot would excuse the terrorist's dealings in death and destruction because it is morally backed by a fatwa. Nor has exemplifying what one society or another across the ages has most highly prized in individuals stopped such individuals from committing atrocities. Indeed, it has all too often been precisely those who have excelled in those qualities that have led men to the slaughter. Yet each approach draws on recognisable strengths. None of us are indifferent to the consequences of conduct and all of us think that happiness is a good. Few would deny the significance of rules in regulating the claims we make on one another. Nor can it be denied that we very much value some personal qualities and scorn others. All such things are factors that quite properly can weigh in making moral judgments. Occasionally they can be at loggerheads, as when a person's action is principled but seems shocking in its disregard of the consequences—or vice versa, welcome in its consequences but unprincipled in its motive. Given the fact that none of the schemes is immune from criticism and each has its value, it should hardly be surprising that moral decision-making is often so vexed an issue. By the same token, understanding the basis on which people make moral decisions, however unselfconsciously they may do so, and having some understanding of the strengths and pitfalls of the things upon which they rely can only improve the situation.

Metaethics

We have explored normative ethical theories, which deal with moral norms by which to regulate conduct or appraise character. Metaethics, by contrast, examines the assumptions and commitments to be found in one or another approach to normative ethics. It deals with such things as the basis of morality, our claims to moral knowledge, and the meaning of moral language. In regard to moral language we have already looked at the terms 'good' and 'right' near the beginning of this chapter, and touched on conceptions of happiness. If space permitted we could explore the meaning of other notions that play a significant role in the moral domain, such as those of reason, motive, justification and excuse. In the space that remains, however, we will limit ourselves to a brief examination of the following three questions:

1. What is the ultimate source of morality and the basis for its claim to authority?
2. How do we come by moral knowledge, if indeed we can claim to know what is good and right?
3. Under what conditions are people to be held morally responsible for what they do?

The basis of morality

If we ask ourselves about the source and authority of moral standards, the traditional line of thought is that it lies with God. Yet we have reason to think that this cannot be sustained. As we saw on p. 46, it is problematic to say that whatever God commanded would be right simply because God commanded it—that murder, for example, would be right if God commanded it. It seems more reasonable to say that God commands what he does because it is right. Once we say this, however, we no longer have an answer as to the ultimate source of moral standards.

The obvious alternative is to move from supernatural authority to worldly authority for moral standards, and say that moral standards are conventions established by society, and that their sanction arises from this and nothing more. This makes morality's source less mysterious, being a matter of history and sociology rather than of theology. Still, there are problems with this view. To say that morality has nothing to appeal to beyond the authority of established social norms implies that moral disputes are little more than power struggles regarding norms and conventions. To some, that may sound plausible. For example, homosexual relations were regarded as immoral by the wider Australian community little more than a generation ago, while these days that is a minority view. And it seems reasonable to say that the change came about as a result of a long struggle against entrenched social mores. All the same, it is important to notice that it was a struggle against discrimination—or, in other words, a battle based on the contention that the prevailing moral standards were wrong. Such a contention wouldn't be possible if the prevailing moral code was the ultimate source of moral authority.

It might be argued that those who fought the battle were merely appealing to other social codes having to do with fairness—that they were insisting on the application of those codes to their case. In the end, however, the problem for the view that the basis of morality is nothing more than social convention comes down to this: While a given moral code might be well entrenched in the society, it seems that we can always sensibly ask whether it is right. If existing moral codes were the final arbiter of what is right there could be no such question.

The problem we just encountered for the view that morality has its basis in nothing more than social norms and conventions looks to be equally a problem for views as diverse as those of Aristotle and Bentham. It can always be meaningfully asked whether character traits that are highly prized by some society (including our own) really are virtuous. And while Bentham equates the good with pleasure, we may question whether pleasure is unequivocally good. This shows that the good cannot be defined as pleasure, or the virtuous in terms of particular character traits, or what's right in terms of established social conventions, other than by stipulation. The fact that people desire pleasure, value certain personal attributes or uphold certain conventions is not sufficient reason to conclude that such things are definitively good, virtuous or right.

This line of thought goes right back to the 18th-century Scottish philosopher David Hume when he remarks that authors writing on morality are in the habit of reasoning from what is and is not the case to what ought or ought not to be so, but that this inference from 'is' to 'ought' is entirely illegitimate. Morality, he says, 'consists not in any *matter of fact*, which can be discover'd by the understanding'. Rather, it is an expression of our feelings. 'So that when you pronounce any action or character to be vicious', says Hume, 'you mean nothing, but that from the constitution of your nature you have a feeling or sentiment of blame from the contemplation of it' (1896, p. 244). This means that there are no facts to be found even in such an act as wilful murder that entitle us to call it vice. To say that murder is abhorrent is simply to express strong feelings against it.

It is one thing to say that the facts of the case by themselves are not sufficient to determine what we ought to do and quite another to say that morality depends upon how we happen to feel about things. It may be that moral standards derive from nothing more than sentiments, and that people unwittingly use such things as divine authority and society's prohibitions as a cloak for their own feelings. Yet is seems clear that, although we may have particular feelings about certain kinds of conduct or personal attributes, it is always legitimate to ask whether those feelings are morally justified. On Hume's own showing, we cannot do so by appealing to the facts. Yet surely there must be something to justify how we feel, if our feelings about such things are indeed justified. Whatever it turns out to be, that will be the ultimate basis of morality.

Moral knowledge

Different views about the basis of morality lead to diverse claims about moral knowledge and how we come by it. Those who base their moral life on religion are likely to say that moral knowledge comes through divine revelation, whether it is found in sacred texts, acquired directly from God or handed down by priests. If one takes a work such as the Bible to be the revealed word of God, for example, then it is being regarded as an unquestionable source of moral knowledge. If one interprets such works as the inspired writings of men who gave us their own understandings as to how we should conduct ourselves, then, of course, no such conclusion can be drawn. Even then, that does not rule out other religious sources of moral knowledge, such as seeking what to do through prayer. One thing that all religious approaches to moral knowledge have in common, however, is their dependence upon faith. Bound up as they are with faith, a religion's claim to provide moral knowledge requires that faith to be justified. That is to say, religion's claims to moral knowledge can be no stronger than faith's claims to knowledge in the first place. That is a central issue in the philosophy of religion.

Utilitarians and pragmatists take moral knowledge to be empirical. According to utilitarians, investigation of the consequences of conduct provides our only source of moral knowledge. If we were to follow Bentham, then we would know that we did the right thing if we can show that what we did produced the best possible balance of pleasure over pain. Similarly, on John Dewey's pragmatic account, our hypotheses as to how we should conduct ourselves are answerable to ongoing investigation into both the causes and the consequences of the things that we currently value. If we can have nothing more than moral hypotheses, that may sound as though we could never have anything that could amount to knowledge. Yet we need to note the parallel with scientific knowledge. The pragmatic scheme treats moral knowledge as being like scientific knowledge—always revisable rather than absolutely certain, and subject to the test of further experience.

While the likes of Bentham are what in philosophy are known as *empiricists*, Kant is what is called a *rationalist*. He believes that ethical knowledge is acquired through reason rather than by experience. To know whether an action of some kind is your moral duty, says Kant, you need only ask yourself whether you can will everyone to behave like that. If so, you know that you are doing the right thing, regardless of what transpires. No further test of experience is required.

Those who follow in the footsteps of David Hume will take a very different path. If moral judgments are merely expressions of our feelings, then there is, properly speaking, no such thing as moral knowledge. For, whatever else knowledge may be, it involves true or, at least, warranted belief. But according to Hume's way of looking at the matter, to say that an action is morally right or wrong, that an end is morally good or bad or that a character trait is virtuous or vicious is not to put forward a belief for which you can supply a warrant. It is simply to express your like or dislike of it.

Moral responsibility

People can be responsible for all kinds of things for which they are not held to be *morally* responsible. To be responsible for an action is to have been the agent of it. To be *morally* responsible for an action, however, is to be able to be rightly held to account, as in being praised for doing what is right or else being blamed for doing wrong.

A person cannot be morally responsible for something with which they had nothing to do. Yet, suppose they had a hand in it, but their hand was forced. We might still say that they aren't to be held accountable, or at least that there are extenuating circumstances. Again, suppose they did something silly but they meant well or, alternatively, that regardless of what they intended to do they simply hadn't foreseen the consequences. What should we say then? By thinking about such cases, we are beginning to explore the conditions under which people may be held to be morally responsible for what they do (and fail to do).

People cannot be morally responsible for things over which they have no control. If someone lacks capacity, or circumstances conspire to thwart their best efforts, then they are excused. Yet they can be held accountable for losing control or not having control in circumstances where they should have foreseen that eventuality and taken steps to prevent it. We do not excuse a drunken driver who loses control of his vehicle and causes an accident, for example, because he should have taken steps to ensure that he did not end up behind the wheel. Under ordinary circumstances, people who lose control of their temper and lash out are culpable in the same way, because they should have learnt to control their temper. People who are in control in the sense of having power and authority in some matter ordinarily bear the primary responsibility when things go wrong, just as people under their control are to some extent sheltered from blame insofar as they were carrying out their duties. The protection afforded is not absolute, however, and a person who was merely 'following orders' is not thereby automatically absolved of all responsibility in cases of wrongdoing. People can be placed under a great deal of pressure or be manipulated by those who exercise power over them, of course. And this can be a mitigating factor, depending upon the extent to which the people concerned should have been able to resist those who were in control.

We need to take account of a person's knowledge of the circumstances in which they act. If a person knew full well what they were doing, then they are likely to be held accountable. Nor do we excuse people who should have known better. To have failed to properly consider the matter is no excuse, and neither is not knowing or taking into account what a person in such a situation should have known or taken into account. We may make allowances when a person has got hold of the wrong end of the stick, as we say, but the extent to which a person is to be excused or held accountable depends upon how they happened to have gone wrong. To have gone wrong through no fault of your own is a strongly mitigating condition.

A person's intention or motive is a relevant consideration. If they didn't intend to do what they did—if it happened by accident, for example—then they are to be excused or, at least, they are less culpable. But what about when someone meant well even though the result of what they did was regrettable? Questions of what the person knew or should have known can be relevant here in assessing culpability, but the broader issue of motive versus consequences takes us back to the normative theories discussed earlier. For a deontologist, the question of intention is crucial. So long as the person honestly tried to do the right thing—to do their duty by the moral law, as Kant would have it—then they acted morally, and they are not to be condemned because of the consequences. For the teleologist, the consequences cannot be so readily swept aside. If you kept a promise knowing that there were likely to be untoward consequences, for example, then you are culpable when they occur. What is praiseworthy on one account can therefore be a matter for condemnation on the other.

Finally, freedom to choose appears to be a necessary condition for moral responsibility. A person cannot be blamed for doing something if they could not have done otherwise. Of course, people often say that they had no choice when in fact they merely did what was expected of them or caved in under pressure. Some degree of moral responsibility can be assigned in that case. Are people ever truly unable to do otherwise? Here philosophers have argued for very different positions, of which the two most extreme may serve for illustration. On the one hand, the 20th-century French existentialist philosopher Jean-Paul Sartre (1992) insisted that we are always free to do otherwise, no matter what the circumstances. Existential choice is a radical freedom from which there is no escape and we are morally responsible no matter what. On the other hand, so-called *hard determinists* have argued that all our actions are determined and that we can never do otherwise than what in fact we do. In consequence, they insist, the idea that we can ever act of our own free will is a myth. If moral responsibility, in turn, depends upon freely choosing to act as we do, then it too is an illusion. No one is ever morally responsible for anything.

This radical rejection of the whole moral enterprise is not to be dismissed out of hand. It is at least possible that all of our actions result from often hidden causes that fully determine what we do. To many philosophers, the contrary so-called *libertarian* view, that our choices and decisions are uncaused interventions in the world, appears naïve. Still, one may try to hang on to freedom and moral responsibility without rejecting the idea that what we do is determined by everything from hereditary and environmental factors right down to the individual events that impinge upon us and the flow of physio-chemical activity in our brains. One can argue, as *compatibilists* do, that free will is compatible with determinism. To take just one such line of argument, if to act freely is merely to act in accord with your own desires, and not to be constrained to act otherwise, then you act freely whenever you are able to act so as to fulfil your desires, no matter that those desires are themselves the result of other causes that are ultimately beyond your control. It is important to notice that this way of saving moral responsibility depends upon the way that freedom is being defined. Whether it should be defined in that way is, of course, a further question for meta-ethical debate.

References

Aristotle, *The Nichomachean ethics*, book 1, trans. WD Ross, available at <http://classics.mit.edu/Aristotle/nicomachaen.html>.

Bentham, J 2007, *An introduction to the principles of morals and legislation*, Dover Publications, New York.

Dewey, J 1957 (1919), *Reconstruction in philosophy*, enlarged edn, Beacon Press, Boston.

Durant, W 1939, *The life of Greece*, Simon & Schuster, New York.

Hume, D 1896 (1739), *A treatise of human nature*, ed. LA Selby-Bigge, Clarendon Press, Oxford. Available at <http://search-ebooks.eu/a-treatise-of-human-nature-258784030>.

Kant, I 1964 (1785), *Groundwork of the metaphysics of morals*, trans. HJ Paton, Harper Torchbooks, New York.

Mill, JS 2008 (1863), *On liberty and other essays*, Oxford University Press.

Nozick, R 1974, *Anarchy, state and utopia*, Basic Books, New York.

Russell, B 1961 (1945), *A history of Western philosophy*, George Allen & Unwin, London.

Sartre, J-P 1992 (1943), *Being and nothingness*, Washington Square Press, New York.

PART TWO

CHAPTER 4

A guide to teaching ethics

Having argued for a collaborative ethical inquiry approach to moral education, and said something about the subject matter of ethics, the time has come to see what is involved in classroom practice. There are two essential aspects to this way of proceeding: collaboration and ethical inquiry. While these two aspects are integrated in the classroom, it is easier to gain an initial understanding of what is involved by looking at the rudiments of ethical inquiry before focussing on the collaborative learning process. There is an underlying pattern to ethical inquiry, and if you familiarise yourself with it at the outset, then you will be more able to follow it in action and have a far better idea of how to construct appropriate classroom activities.

The basic pattern of ethical inquiry

The basic pattern of ethical inquiry can be represented in a flowchart that breaks down the inquiry process into a sequence of operations, each of which has a distinctive function within the overall undertaking. I will elaborate upon components of the flowchart as we proceed.

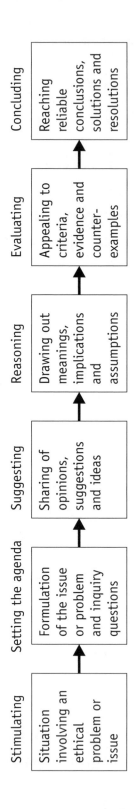

The basic pattern of ethical inquiry

Stimulating

Situation involving an ethical problem or issue

Setting the agenda

Formulation of the issue or problem and inquiry questions

Suggesting

Sharing of opinions, suggestions and ideas

Reasoning

Drawing out meanings, implications and assumptions

Evaluating

Appealing to criteria, evidence and counter-examples

Concluding

Reaching reliable conclusions, solutions and resolutions

Stimulating ethical inquiry

Ethical inquiry doesn't occur through spontaneous combustion. Something needs to kindle it. In order to appreciate this, we have only to think about familiar inquiries outside of the classroom. Suppose you haven't been feeling very well and that prompts you to visit your doctor. The doctor's questions and clinical observations may result in a diagnosis, but it is also possible that the doctor may not be sure of the cause of your symptoms and further tests may be required. In other words, the doctor may need to pursue a line of inquiry. The particular point to note, however, is that this inquiry was initiated because of worries about your health. Concern over your symptoms motivated you to act. Without that, the inquiry would not have occurred. Similar stories could be told about taking your car to the motor mechanic, detectives being called to the scene of a crime or governments setting up a commission of inquiry into some serious issue that has arisen in society. In practical matters, inquiry does not begin unless there is some issue or problem to motivate it.

Although classroom ethical inquiry is not generally designed to settle immediate moral issues and problems, it is ultimately concerned with how we should conduct ourselves in regard to such matters. It is therefore in need of situations, issues and problems that will provoke inquiry into matters of character and conduct. In other words, if we want to encourage ethical inquiry in the classroom, then we will need matters of genuine ethical concern to students in order to motivate it. Whether the stimulus is topical, is raised by fiction, relates to history or concerns the uses of science and technology—no matter the subject matter to which it is connected—it needs to be presented in such a way that students will be drawn to it and want to ask questions about it.

We must take care not to set things up so as to presume the answers to such questions. If we do so, we are undercutting the motivation to inquire. For a simple illustration of the point, consider Aesop's fables. These stories have delighted countless generations of children and their literary merit is not in doubt. Since they deal with morals, they might seem a natural choice for ethical exploration through a primary school reading program. Otherwise excellent though they may be, the problem is that these stories are constructed to draw a moral. They are designed to be morally instructive. That makes them unsuitable for ethical inquiry.

By contrast, consider the picture book *It's So Unfair* by Pat Thomson (2005), in which a farmer's wife sweeps a cat out of the farmhouse after it has committed a long list of misdemeanours. The cat's cries that this is so unfair are echoed by one farmyard animal after another as the cat successively reveals all the naughty things it did. Incensed by what happened to the cat, the animals complain to the farmer, who agrees that the cat has been unfairly treated and invites it back into the house. But when the cat reveals that, in addition to all the things that upset the farmer's wife, it also made a puddle on the farmer's favourite chair, he immediately shoos it out again. 'That's just *so* unfair', the cat protests, to cries of sympathy from the farmyard animals. Unlike Aesop's fables, Thomson's story is not constructed so as to draw a moral. Instead, it problematises the notion of fairness. It is therefore likely to raise issues and questions about fair treatment in the minds of young students that can form a basis for ethical inquiry.

Setting the agenda

It is one thing to set ethical issues and problems for students and another to present them with material that provokes them to raise these things themselves. The latter is a more natural starting point for ethical inquiry and builds the capacity to discern ethical issues and problems. To appreciate the importance of this fact we only need keep in mind that in everyday life ethical problems and issues do not come already marked out in textbook fashion. We need to identify and articulate them for ourselves. So students should typically be required to identify the ethical issues and problems embedded in the stimulus material rather than being given them directly.

Once we are confronted by an ethical problem or issue, we then face questions about what to do. The answer to such questions may be obvious, but if there are different possible responses open to us and we are uncertain as to which path to take, or if they admit of various opinions or different points of view, then we need to *inquire* as to where we should stand or what we should do. In the same vein, students need to ask appropriate questions in order to focus their inquiries and set their agenda. In this context, a question can be thought of as a probe. By asking probing questions, students are attempting to put their finger on something of interest and importance—on some significant aspect of an ethical problem or issue that they are wondering about and which they would like to explore. The art of asking just the right questions—ones that go to the heart of some matter—can only be cultivated through practice. We should not presume that students can do this at the outset or that it can be taught in a lesson or two. Like any art, developing the ability to question requires persistent effort.

Since to inquire is first and foremost to question, and to question is to inquire, students must learn the art of questioning if they are going to develop their capacity to inquire into ethical matters. I cannot stress this too strongly. There is nothing wrong with helping to strengthen students' inquiries by supplementing their questions, of course, but if we simply supply them with questions of our own, then we are failing to develop one of the most basic skills of inquiry, as well as undercutting a valuable source of motivation.

Suggesting

Once a question is under discussion, ethical inquiry invites students to respond with suggestions. Suggestions include the expression of many kinds of thoughts. Propositions can be put, guesses made, meanings conjectured, explanations proposed and so on. All such suggestions have a tentative quality. They are offerings that require examination; things to be put to the test.

It is common to offer a suggestion by saying that we have an *idea*. In the context of ethical inquiry, an idea is just that—a hint or inkling of a way forward, or a notion that may prove to be fruitful in addressing a question. Ideas therefore function in the manner of suggestions, and just as one suggestion may be met by another, so one idea may be followed by another, indicating different possible ways of dealing with some matter or of understanding it.

In conducting ethical inquiry in the classroom it is absolutely essential for the expression of students' opinions to be treated as suggestions. In other contexts people all too frequently defend their opinion by attacking any contrary opinion, or by more forcefully reasserting their opinion if challenged. It is therefore of vital importance for students to come to realise that their opinions are valued in ethical inquiry as thoughts that are worth sharing because they are worth thinking about and not necessarily because they are right. When faced with contrary opinions, inquirers do not simply stand on their digs. If it turns out that there is more to be said for a different opinion, they are more likely to change their minds than to stand their ground.

Reasoning about suggestions

In order to understand the import of suggestions, we need to see what follows from them, whether as a matter of likely consequences or of logical implication. Reasoning is the drawing of such inferences. While few teachers have any formal training in reasoning or logic, all teachers can detect obvious signs of illogicality in their students. We need to pay careful attention to students' reasoning because there is a price to be paid for reasoning poorly. People draw inferences when they should not, or fail to do so when they should. Then they act, or fail to do so, and suffer the consequences. While this is not just a problem in the moral domain, its consequences there are all too familiar. Those whose powers of reasoning are weak are prone to make ill-supported moral judgments. Or again, those who are not in the habit of reasoning about moral matters are much more likely to approach moral disputes in other ways. Going off in a huff, verbal abuse and violence are familiar enough, as is the resulting breakdown of relationships.

To explore the practical implications of action is to more fully understand its import, just as to examine the logical implications of a statement is to more completely grasp its meaning. Failure to appreciate the likely consequences of our actions can land us in all sorts of strife that might have been prevented. Failure to see what follows from a statement results in the shallow grasp of all kinds of content that is so often lamented by teachers. These facts alone provide sufficient grounds to develop students' capacities to reason.

Reasoning can also uncover assumptions upon which suggestions depend. It is often useful to see what is being taken for granted, especially when it turns out that a suggestion is premised on a dubious assumption. The suggestion that someone ought to have repaid a kindness, for example, may be put forward on the assumption that one good turn deserves another. If so, it would be worth uncovering this principle and examining whether it is universally applicable or appropriate in the circumstances.

Evaluating suggestions

We reason about suggestions in ethical inquiry in order to evaluate them. Students who draw attention to the negative consequences of what they see as unethical conduct are likely to be providing grounds for their claim. The same is true if they argue that a course of action is objectionable because it is inconsistent with what they take to be an established moral principle. Students may also draw attention to the fact that a suggestion follows only upon certain assumptions which they believe to be shaky. In many such ways, ethical inquiry involves students in evaluating their own suggestions by reasoning about them.

Students' suggestions often contain key concepts whose meanings need to be explored. A student who responds to the suggestion by saying that it all depends upon what is meant by a crucial term—'free', say, or what is meant by 'good'—is drawing attention to an ethical concept. In ethics we employ many such concepts. We are concerned with the concepts of *right* and *wrong*, with *goodness, justice, fairness* and *discrimination*, with *happiness, honesty, tolerance* and *friendship*, to name but a few. One of the most productive ways of exploring these key concepts—or what for younger students we may simply call these 'big ideas'—is to discover the criteria that govern their application. That is to say, to ask ourselves on what grounds we may say that something we are considering is, for instance, fair or not fair. The reasons supplied are, or point to, tentative criteria for saying that something is fair or not. They provide an initial assemblage of criteria that can then be modified and put into order. Through this process of conceptual exploration, students are led to a deeper understanding of the concepts being used. And they are thereby able to make better judgments—not just in the case in question, but in any case that relies upon the application of those concepts.

As in other areas of inquiry, the evaluation of suggestions in ethical inquiry depends upon an appeal to reason and evidence. It is important to recognise, however, that those who subscribe to different ethical theories are likely to resort to different kinds of appeal. Even before students become aware of these theories, their attempts at evaluation are likely to reflect this divergence. Students who are inclined to point to the consequences of actions in order to evaluate them, for instance, are taking an implicitly consequentialist or teleological stance. Those who are more inclined to evaluate actions by reference to independently established principles, by contrast, are your budding deontologists. Teachers therefore need to have a basic knowledge of ethical theory in order to detect these different moves when students make them and stay on top of the discussion.

Students are often inclined to use personal experience for illustration and evidential support. So long as this does not involve inappropriate revelation (e.g. private family matters) or lapses into anecdote, this is a good thing. It means that students are trying to make sense of what they are learning in the classroom in terms of their experience and their world.

While making this connection is of value in other areas of education, it is of vital import in moral education. Moral education that does not connect with the experience and life-world of students fails in its task.

There is a special kind of example used for evaluative purposes in ethical inquiry. This is what is known as a *counterexample*. Counterexamples are examples that run counter to general claims. So when students rely upon unwarranted generalisations, for instance, they need to be brought up against an example or two to show that their generalisation is problematic. The same applies to principles or rules of conduct that students put forward. It is often worth asking whether students can come up with any potential counterexamples that might lead them to think further about such suggestions.

Reaching conclusions

While ethical inquiry may result in a wide variety of conclusions, it is fair to say that they centre on values. This includes the conclusion that certain things are good, or better than others, and that certain actions are right (or wrong) or more (or less) acceptable than others. Traditional moral and values education provides instruction as to what students ought to value. It maintains that certain actions are right, while others are wrong, and that some things are good, while others are not so. This may be done by a number of means, such as laying down the rules and enforcing conduct, appealing to higher authority and leading by example. While these things have their place, ethical inquiry takes another approach because it has a different purpose. It aims to inform and improve reasoning and judgment in regard to ethical issues and problems through the careful consideration of them. It employs the various ways of thinking about such matters that significant moral thinkers have bequeathed to us, and develops students' capacities to think in these ways. Given this, it is not the aim of ethical inquiry that students should all come to a given conclusion. They may well do so, but that is not what we are striving to achieve. If you insist, however implicitly, that the students' inquiry should come to a pre-set judgment or conclusion, then the inquiry cannot be a search for the truth. It cannot be genuine. Students will spot this very quickly and rightly be turned off by it.

This does not mean that you should never challenge conclusions that students are tempted to draw. On the contrary, it is first and foremost your responsibility to question students if they fail to consider significant alternatives, engage in sloppy reasoning, acquiesce in superficial under-standing or fall prey to any of the multitude of sins that come under the head of poor thinking. Provided that students arrive at conclusions that are well thought out and adequately justified, the inquiry will have achieved its overall aim, in terms of both the thinking process and whatever substantive conclusions may have been drawn.

A couple of points are worth stressing here. One is that different members of the class may come to different conclusions. Given that people do not always agree with one another about ethical matters in the broader community, we should not be surprised to find that we do not always achieve unanimity in the classroom. Moreover, it can be salutary for students to learn by experience that people can sometimes come to different conclusions in ethical matters for perfectly good reasons. It helps to develop a sense of moral humility and breeds tolerance. The other point is that it runs contrary to the spirit of inquiry for its conclusions to be held dogmatically, as if there were no possibility of our having misjudged the matter. We should be willing to admit our fallibility in moral matters and not assume that we have godlike powers of moral discernment. Ethical inquiry should furnish us with judgments that are reasonable and reliable. To claim that they are reasonable is to say that they are supported by adequate reasons or evidence. To claim that they are reliable is to say that we can depend upon them. But we would be ill-advised to rule out the possibility that factors may come to light that render our previous judgments less reasonable than we had supposed and to therefore question the extent to which we may rely upon them.

* * *

This completes my sketch of the basic pattern of inquiry. Before shading in its collaborative dimension, I need to guard against a possible misunderstanding. Up to this point, I may have given the impression that ethical inquiry always proceeds in a linear fashion from one phase to the next. The truth is that I have presented it this way only for ease of exposition. Ethical inquiry more typically involves back-and-forth movements between its phases. The reasons for this are not hard to find. A question may turn out not to be sufficiently clear, for instance, and students may need to go back and clarify the question after having made some faltering attempts to address it. Again, when the implications of a suggestion lead to a negative evaluation, students may find themselves returning to some alternative that was mentioned earlier. Many such kinds of toing and froing can be necessary for the inquiry to successfully move forwards overall. Once again, it is your responsibility to ensure that any backtracking is appropriate and to keep the inquiry on the rails with judicious questioning as necessary. That responsibility can gradually be ceded to students as they internalise the inquiry process, but you should not be too quick to remove the scaffolding that supports the learner.

Making ethical inquiry collaborative

Ethical inquiry involves many kinds of thinking. Notable among these are identifying and describing a problem or issue, constructing questions, developing suggestions and ideas, inferring logical and practical consequences, identifying assumptions, appealing to criteria, weighing reasons and evidence, constructing counterexamples and drawing conclusions. Some of these are examples of critical thinking, while others are more creative. To appeal to criteria in order to justify a claim, for instance, or to weigh up one reason against another is to exercise critical judgment. Coming up with ideas and imagining counterexamples, on the other hand, are creative acts. In addition to both critical and creative thinking, however, there is a third kind of thinking that is of particular relevance to moral education and therefore to be encouraged in ethical inquiry. It builds on the acknowledgement that thinking about things such as values is not a dispassionate, purely cerebral affair and that moral education should involve what has been called 'caring thinking' (see Lipman 1995, 2003 and Noddings 2003). As I see it, caring thinking focuses on the social aspect of thinking—an aspect that comes to the fore when students are thinking together.

The common conception of thinking in education is well represented by Rodin's famous sculpture, *The Thinker*. A solitary individual with his head upon his hand and a pensive gaze, Rodin's thinker inwardly ponders some problem or issue. He is the personification of thinking as internal ratiocination. This conception contrasts sharply with the image of thinking found in Raphael's painting, *The School of Athens*. At the centre of the picture Plato and Aristotle can be seen debating as to whether we should inquire into the things of this world or contemplate an otherworldly reality. Around them many other groups of thinkers are engaged in discussion. Raphael presents us with thinking in its discursive form.

Although Raphael's vision of thinkers is a less iconic image than Rodin's individual, it is more fitting for students involved in ethical inquiry in the classroom. Such thinkers are not just occupied with subject matter. They are also engaged with one another. In discussion, thinkers speak and listen. For them, thought is bound up with verbal articulation and active listening, with communicating with and comprehending one another. They respond to one another by building on each other's contributions. They question one another, offer support and criticism, suggest alternative lines of inquiry and put forward different points of view. Thinking in its social form is communicative rather than inwardly contained and transmutes the private processes of the solitary thinker into interpersonal exchange.

One of the distinctive things about such thinking is the need for the participants to cooperate with one another. A few examples should make this clear.

- Vanessa helps Andrew to improve his question.
- Sensing that others have misunderstood what Rachel was trying to say, Jamal attempts to clarify her remarks.
- Jeremy makes it clear that he is disagreeing with Roberto's suggestion and not criticising him.
- Even though he passionately disagrees with Ingrid, Asad stops himself from interrupting her and listens carefully to what she is saying.

These are examples of caring thinking. They are as vital a part of collaborative ethical inquiry as is critical and creative thinking. They involve thinking tempered by moral regard for one another as well as for the inquiry. This means that, when infused with caring thinking, ethical inquiry becomes a form of ethical practice in itself. That's as it should be if the inquiry is to be carried out in a manner that properly reflects its subject matter. Ironically, discussions of moral matters outside of the classroom are all too often displays of poor behaviour—something for which an ethical education that involves caring thinking can help to supply a remedy.

Having introduced the topic of collaboration, let us now revisit the various phases of the inquiry process to see what they look like when carried out in this mode.

Stimulating ethical inquiry

Collaborative ethical inquiry needs more than just an appropriate shared stimulus. It requires the kind of setting in which students will be motivated to discuss ethical problems and issues. This includes a classroom atmosphere that invites inquiry as well as a physical setup that facilitates rather than hinders collaboration.

A classroom where students are anxious about speaking, because they are worried about giving the wrong answer, or about being ridiculed for saying what they think, can hardly be expected to promote ethical inquiry. Students need to know that in ethical inquiry we are not dealing with settled right answers but with problems, issues and questions in response to which there may be a number of suggestions that are worth discussing.

Even at the end of the day, the conclusions we come to might not be final and agreed to by all, as there may be more than one defensible possibility or point of view.

Class discussion should form an integral part of collaborative ethical inquiry, and it is best promoted when the students can see one another face-to-face, and when the teacher is not standing at the front of the class. This is vital. It is your role to facilitate an orderly, thoughtful discussion among the students—not to lead it—and this requires students to be able to address one another without craning around. The natural formation for collaborative inquiry is a circle. It facilitates exchange between students and enables them to pick up on non-verbal cues. While you are likely to need access to a whiteboard or an easel, this does not prevent you from sitting at some convenient point in the circle.

To facilitate class discussion, particularly in ensuring that only one person speaks at a time, it is a good idea to introduce a Speaker's Ball. This means that the person with the ball is the speaker and everyone else is a listener. Something large like a basketball is best so that the ball can be easily rolled between students rather than thrown. With a large ball, the speakers can also fold their hands on top of the ball when they have finished speaking. In this way, the class is not distracted by people with their hands up while someone is speaking.

Collaborative ethical inquiry also lends itself to small group work, which once again is likely to involve a good deal of discussion. In fact, moving between class discussion and break-out groups is often a good strategy for structuring discussion. For example, if you are aware that there are many students who are keen to have an input at some point in a whole class discussion, then breaking into small groups (or even discussing the matter with their neighbour) and reporting back to the class can be a very productive move, and alleviates the frustration that otherwise may be felt by students who are trying to get a turn. Breaking momentarily into small groups can also provide a fillip to the inquiry by allowing a range of views to surface and then be fed back into the class discussion when it resumes. Just the additional talking time made available to each student by small group discussion and work in pairs increases engagement.

Setting the agenda

When we introduce stimulus material in order to initiate ethical inquiry, we are asking for students to raise issues or problems and related questions that they can go on to address. We can either start by asking students what ethical issues or problems the material raises and then have the students ask questions about them, or first go to questions and then get the students to group those questions into topics. While we can do this on the basis of individual student responses, it is often better to make use of group work. By dividing the class into small groups and asking them to identify an issue or construct a question, we provoke cooperative discussion. Different students may identify different issues or see them differently. They are likely to come up with different questions, or attempt to frame them differently. If they have been asked to come up with just one important issue, say, or to produce one really good ethical question for discussion, then the adjudication between their different responses will ultimately result in more incisive descriptions and better questions.

Again, suppose that you have called for individuals to raise issues and recorded their responses on the board. Then it can be profitable to divide the class into small groups and have each group construct a question about a selected issue. The same applies if a set of questions has been recorded on the board and students are formed into small groups in order to discuss whether some of the questions have significant connections so that they can be grouped together.

Finally, if you have a surfeit of issues or questions, it is often a good idea to ask the students which one or ones they are most keen to explore. A vote, for example, may reveal that the centre of student interest is not where you took it to be. Don't be overly concerned if the students want to discuss some topic other than the one you would have chosen. Make good use of their interest to start them thinking. You can always come back to the other topic later on.

If you start with an ethical problem or issue be sure to extract a clear statement of it from the students before you move on, and get it up on the board so that everyone can see it. Go on to list any questions that may have been provoked. If you have put students in groups and asked them to construct a thought-provoking question about some issue, then supply each group with a felt pen and a large sheet of paper so that you can display their questions on the board. Regardless of the starting point, the issue or question being addressed needs to be kept clearly in sight as you proceed.

Suggestions

The value of the inquiry being collaborative is easy to see when it comes to working with students' suggestions. Inquiry involves choosing between different possible paths as we find our way forward, and suggestions are the various proposals that point down those pathways. In ethics, this involves such things as selecting between different possible ways of dealing with a situation, choosing between different ethical principles, relying upon different values or adjudicating between different points of view regarding a person's character or conduct. The fact that students come to ethical inquiry with different opinions and points of view, that they may already rely upon different implicit principles, have somewhat different values and appraise other people's conduct and character differently, is all grist to the mill. It helps to supply a ready source of suggestions which can then be thought through.

Having a variety of suggestions brings students to reflect upon whatever they happen to think and to consider the alternatives provided by their peers. This means adjudicating between alternative suggestions, and it is this weighing and considering, this deliberation, which builds both the disposition to make considered moral judgments and the capacity to do that well. The fact that these results are achieved through collaborative effort also means that when students face conflicts with one another, they will be more inclined, as well as better able, to be reasonable with one another and to find more amicable resolutions of their difficulties.

In beginning to address an ethical issue, problem or question it is best to ask students for suggestions. Whether you take a number of suggestions before getting the students to explore any of them in depth depends upon the situation. Often that is best, but sometimes it is preferable to explore one possibility before turning to another. In whatever way you go, it is advisable to keep track of progress on the board, with the various suggestions linking up to the problem or question that is being addressed.

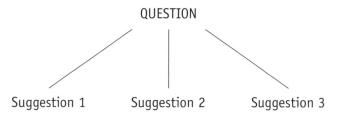

This is the beginning of what I call a Discussion Map (see Cam 2006, pp. 82–85). As the various suggestions are evaluated or explored, the map will be extended, so be sure to allow plenty of room.

Reasoning

Reasoning is inference-making. It is the drawing of conclusions from premises. While this is something that may happen at any stage in an ethical inquiry, its primary application revolves around the implications of suggestions—implications that students will need to grasp in order to understand and evaluate those suggestions. Let us look at reasoning in its collaborative mode.

Assumptions provide a convenient starting point. An assumption is a premise that is needed to support a proposition, or what we have been calling a suggestion. When an assumption is questionable or dubious it should be unearthed. The trouble is that individuals are not likely to be aware of questionable assumptions that may lie behind their own suggestions. Others who have already rejected that idea, or who mull over what is being put to them, are far more likely to spot them. Far from this being combative, as it would be in debate, when students engage in collaborative inquiry they come to rely upon others to uncover weaknesses in their contributions so as to correct and improve them. This does not mean that someone in the class is bound to spot a doubtful assumption, of course, and you may need to intervene on occasion to help bring it out. Rather than directly pointing out the fault, however, it is better to ask the class what is being assumed, or, if need be, to ask the student whose suggestion is under discussion whether they are making that assumption, without explicitly indicating that it is problematic. In other words, do your best to allow the students to see for themselves that questionable assumptions are being made.

To examine the likely consequences of adopting a suggestion is to consider its import, just as to point out the logical implications of a proposition is to analyse its meaning. Let's take an example. The suggestion that it is wrong to kill whales because they are mammals implicitly relies upon the claim (or *assumes*) that it is wrong to kill mammals. In effect, the underlying reasoning goes as follows:

Whales are mammals.

It is wrong to kill mammals.

Therefore: It is wrong to kill whales.

By the same reasoning, of course, a person who held to that view would also have to accept that it is wrong to kill cattle, sheep and pigs. While such a person may be prepared to accept the consequences of this policy, others may be less happy with them, for a variety of reasons. Even so, those who argue that there is nothing wrong with beef, lamb and pork remaining on the table are forced to deny that it is wrong to kill mammals.

It is easy to see this little vignette unfolding in the classroom. Suppose that a discussion about whaling is just getting underway when Tom claims that it is wrong to kill whales. When his classmates press him for a reason, he says that it is wrong to kill whales because whales are mammals.

'So,' says Tien, 'you're implying that it's wrong to kill mammals.'

'That's right,' Tom replies.

'Well,' asks Tien, 'what about sheep? They're mammals and we kill them.'

'And cows and pigs,' says Nicky—and so on it goes. Here the reasoning process is driven by the dialogue between the participants. It is different from the monological construction of an argument by an individual. It does not involve simply taking a stand, but reasoning about the issue from different points of view.

Make sure to note any significant reasoning about a suggestion on the Discussion Map. If doubtful assumptions are raised, then flag them. List any noteworthy implications and be on the lookout for both good and bad reasoning. If an example of good reasoning occurs, it may be worth interrupting the discussion to reconstruct it on the board. The same is true of dubious reasoning. By reconstructing it on the board, the error is more likely to become apparent to the class. In any event, do not let poor reasoning go by unchecked.

Evaluating

In evaluating suggestions students engage in the give and take of reasons. In the fragment sketched above about whaling, Tom gave 'being mammals' as a reason for his claim that it is wrong to kill whales. Regardless of whether Tom's reason is a good one, it is an attempt to support his claim, just as Tien and Nicky's rejoinders are meant to raise questions about it. The combination of Tom's reason-giving and their reasoning provide the beginnings of a collaborative evaluation. In fact, both Tom and the girls are relying upon the same pattern of reasoning. As Tien implies, if Tom's reason was a good one, it would be wrong to kill sheep:

> Sheep are mammals.
> It is wrong to kill mammals.
> *Therefore*: It is wrong to kill sheep.

Here Tien and then Nicky are relying upon the fact that we kill other mammals. So how can it be wrong to kill whales just because they are mammals? That's hardly the end of the matter, of course. The mere fact that we do kill sheep doesn't make it alright.

In dealing with reasoning and evaluation, it is important to distinguish justification from inference. Sometimes the two are confused when we talk about reasoning and reason-giving. In evaluating, we give reasons primarily in order to justify or cast doubt upon some claim or suggestion. In reasoning, we make inferences or draw conclusions, and for the purposes of evaluation this is once again primarily in order to justify a claim (as in Tom's reasoning above) or to question it (as Tien and Nicky do). In order to make it clear to everyone what move they are making, it is worth starting out by insisting that students use the word 'because' to mark the fact that they are giving a reason and to use 'therefore' to mark an inference to a conclusion—or, less happily, for young children to use 'so'.

Once reason-giving has been clearly distinguished from reasoning in this way, it is worth ensuring that students come to realise that justification and inference are related. They are the reverse of one another. In order to see this we need only rework the example that was given:

> *Justification*: Killing whales is wrong *because* whales are mammals and it is wrong to kill mammals.
> *Inference*:   Whales are mammals. It is wrong to kill mammals. *Therefore*, it is wrong to kill whales.

Primary school students can learn to make both of these moves and, with practice, they will be able to move freely backwards and forwards between them. In fact, this backwards and forwards movement is to be expected in collaborative ethical inquiry. When Tom suggested that it is wrong to kill whales *because* they are mammals, Tien immediately saw that this is a good reason only if it is wrong to kill mammals. In other words, Tien saw that Tom needs this general proposition in order to support his contention— that he cannot *draw the conclusion* that it is wrong to kill whales without this additional premise. She then suggests that by the same reasoning we can conclude that it's wrong to kill sheep. Since Tien doesn't think that it is wrong to kill sheep, she takes this to be a *counterexample* to Tom's claim. Of course, this leaves it open to Tom to maintain that it is wrong to kill sheep precisely because they are mammals; but at this stage he will need some further reason (some further *because*) as to why it is wrong to kill mammals.

As elsewhere, the appeal to criteria provides an important means of evaluation in ethics. This includes such things as accepted standards of conduct, principles, measures of wellbeing and harm and appeal to values like happiness and fairness. It is vital to note, however, that conformity to accepted criteria does not necessarily provide an incontestable verdict in the context of inquiry. The mere fact that something is accepted does not automatically make it acceptable. While conformity to principles is a common form of evaluation in ethics, principles sometimes admit of exceptions, and acting on one principle may bring it into conflict with another, as well as with other measures of morality such as preventing harm. And what constitutes such things as happiness and fairness is nearly always contestable.

Nowhere is this clearer than in collaborative ethical inquiry: Ravi claims that certain practices in another culture are wrong because they do not respect human rights, while Abdul defends them as part of a time-honoured way of life. Sarah thinks that you should always tell the truth, regardless of the consequences, while Callum believes that there are cases where avoiding potential harm requires us to be less than frank. Billy thinks it would be fair if everyone were given the same size serving of birthday cake, whereas Jonathon argues that bigger people should be given bigger pieces of cake than littler people. Evaluating these competing claims cannot be just a matter of appealing to a criterion that may itself be in dispute. Sorting out contesting claims can also require us to examine and defend our criteria.

Reason and evidence are a means of evaluation in ethical inquiry as they are in any inquiry. Such things as contradiction or inconsistency, dubious assumptions and susceptibility to counterexamples are every bit as important as pointing to untoward consequences or the presentation of revealing illustrations. Yet there is no getting away from the fact that whereas the weight placed upon a body of evidence may be debatable, logical considerations are not. For students to contradict themselves, or to draw conclusions that simply do not follow, is to go wrong in the same kind of way that they can go wrong in maths. It is to commit a logical mistake that needs correction. Once again, it is best for students to correct their own breaches of reason, but if they fail to do so then the teacher needs to draw attention to them.

By contrast, it is possible for someone to stick to their view in ethics even in the face of what appears to other students to be overwhelming evidence against it. For example, in the previous chapter we encountered the Kantian claim that it is wrong to tell a lie, no matter what. When presented with an example in which the consequences of telling the truth may be quite untoward, a student who took this view would still say that you should tell the truth. They would stand in need of justification for doing so, of course, whether of the kind that Kant gives, or some other. As such an example dramatically illustrates, however, the facts do not simply speak for themselves in ethics. They must contend with principles and other general considerations that are brought to bear.

When it comes to ethics, the interpretation of evidence is also a somewhat subjective affair. In order to appreciate this, we only need reflect on the varied reactions that different people often have to the same behaviour or character traits of a third party. What I take to be rude, you may see as forthright. I look upon someone as being stubborn, while you take them to show determination. The same applies to the interpretation of character and conduct in literature, for exactly the same reasons. We do not perceive others with clinical detachment but through the lens of our own make-up. This fact is an inevitable feature of collaborative ethical inquiry, where the various participants' judgments about conduct and character are constantly in play. Even so, as in the study of literature, students of ethics are learning to make better supported assessments of such things. While there is obviously no single correct interpretation of the characters of Shylock or King Lear, there can be more or less perceptive as well as amply or flimsily supported assessments of such things, as any secondary school English teacher knows only too well. In this respect, the beauty of collaborative ethical inquiry is its considerable capacity to help hone the critical capacities of students to make better judgments, and to deepen their understandings of character and conduct, including their own.

Concluding

Inquiry into questions about the moral life tends to be open-ended in the sense that whatever conclusions we reach are nearly always subject to revision in the light of subsequent experience or the dawning of further insight. This does not mean that no progress can be made. Indeed, students will be frustrated, not to mention short-changed, if the lesson does not result in a demonstrable outcome in relation to the subject matter. There must be a sense that the lesson has resulted in progress with whatever is under discussion. Looking back, students should be able to see that they have squarely tackled an ethical problem or issue, that they have asked pertinent questions about it, and have explored and evaluated a range of suggestions. This may mean that they have got a better grip on the problem, or that they have managed to see it from a different perspective. It can mean that they have become aware that there are serious questions about some matter that deserve further consideration, or that questions they would have answered without a second thought are more complicated than they took them to be. It can also be that they have seen why certain responses to an issue are problematic, or, instead, that they have confirmed what they thought all along for perfectly good reasons that are now all the more apparent to them. In short, the results of the inquiry into a given subject matter can be many and various, and not every student is likely to come to the same conclusion. But conclusions there must be, even if they are sometimes tentative or diverse.

Collaborative ethical inquiry seldom goes straight. It tacks back and forth as the students venture a suggestion, critique it and then try another tack. This pattern of going in one direction and then self-correcting and setting another course is likely to be repeated over and again in the conduct of an inquiry. Yet it should result in forward movement overall. The teacher needs to ensure that the students' evaluation of each other's suggestions results in this kind of progress and, as the discussion builds, to make students mindful of what is achieved. This requires the teacher to help the students keep their bearings, which can be difficult unless the teacher lays down some markers. As I suggested earlier, you would be well advised to keep track of progress by constructing a Discussion Map. If a suggestion was abandoned for good reasons, for example, then an indication of the fact should be plain for all to see. If consideration of the pros and cons of another suggestion only resulted in a further question, then that should be noted too. And ditto if there was an unresolved disagreement in regard to a third suggestion—and so on, however the discussion goes.

Such a map provides the basis for conclusions to be drawn. In the case illustrated, the only established outcome is that Suggestion 1 will not do. It may be that investigation of the question raised in regard to Suggestion 2 will resolve the matter, as might a further examination of the basis for the disagreement over Suggestion 3. Individual students may draw their own

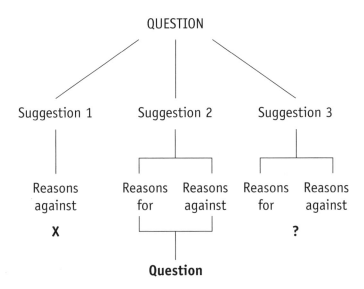

conclusion in regard to Suggestion 3, of course, but they will be well aware that others disagree with them for what appear to those others to be good reasons. While this result is less tidy than those that we conventionally associate with the classroom, such is the nature of most questions worth thinking about in the moral domain. It is therefore a virtue and not a weakness of collaborative ethical inquiry that it is likely to bring this out.

References

Cam, P 1995, *Thinking together: philosophical inquiry for the classroom*, Primary English Teaching Association/Hale & Iremonger, Sydney.

Cam, P 2006, *Twenty thinking tools: collaborative inquiry for the classroom*, ACER Press, Camberwell.

Lipman, M 1995, 'Caring as thinking', *Inquiry: critical thinking across the disciplines*, vol. 15, no. 1, pp. 1–13.

Lipman, M 2003, *Thinking in education*, 2nd edn, Cambridge University Press.

Noddings, N 2003, *Caring: a feminine approach to ethics and moral education*, 2nd edn, University of California Press, Berkeley.

Thomson, P 2005, *It's so unfair*, Anderson Press, London.

CHAPTER 5

Constructing activities and exercises

This chapter introduces you to a range of activities for ethical inquiry. Even though many of the activities provided are likely to be directly useable in your classroom, my intention is not to give you a grab-bag of activities so much as to provide a guide to the construction of activities so that you can devise them for yourself. I am confident that you will be able to use the models provided to develop activities to suit your own purposes.

Rather than laying out ethical subject matter in terms of curriculum areas or levels of schooling, I have constructed activities around three central planks of collaborative ethical inquiry: questioning, conceptual exploration and reasoning. I have also provided background information about the activities where that is needed in order to understand the role they can play in an inquiry-based approach to moral education.

In addition to the activity base, I have included some exercises in reasoning. By an exercise, I mean a task that targets a specific skill, such as uncovering an assumption, identifying a pattern of reasoning or spotting a fallacy. Such exercises provide a useful adjunct to class discussion and small group work, which forms the mainstay of collaborative ethical inquiry. The skills they develop enable students to think more carefully about ethical issues.

Questioning

While traditional moral education relies upon instruction rather than reflection, an inquiring approach to these matters very much depends on the capacity of students to probe and to question. This is not to say that the teacher should avoid plying students with questions. That is often needful, and I deal with such teacher-supplied topic questions under 'Constructing Discussion Plans' beginning on p. 104. At the outset, however, it is important to stress that such questions should not become a substitute for having students construct questions. The ability of students to raise their own questions is indispensible in developing an intelligent approach to issues and problems in the moral domain. Hence I will begin with some activities that aim to develop the art of questioning in students.

The student as questioner

Although young children can be full of questions, they do not necessarily know how to ask an appropriate question as a task demand. This is something that we need to teach them. Here is a basic scaffolding technique that will enable students in the early years to learn to ask what we may call 'Big Questions' suitable for collaborative ethical inquiry when provided with a stimulus such as a picture book. The exact procedure may vary with the character of the book, but the following will serve to give you the general idea.

Activity: Big Questions

Procedure
After reading the story, ask students the following three questions (or similar ones, as appropriate to the material) and record the responses:

1. What were you thinking about when you were listening to that story?
2. Were there things that you liked about how the characters behaved in the story? What things were they?
3. Were there things that you didn't like about how the characters behaved in the story? What were they?

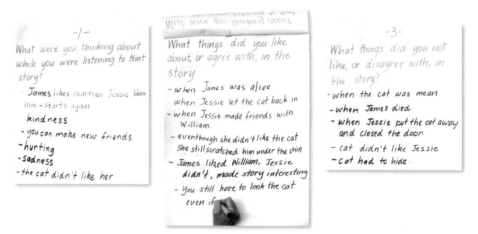

Underline the key words used by the children that would be suitable to ask a question about. The children then ask their Big Questions.[1]

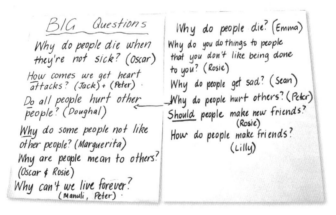

Photographs courtesy of Buranda State School, Brisbane.

1   Modelled on 'Ask Three Questions' in Cam et al. 2007.

This is a time-consuming procedure, as you can see, but it pays handsome dividends. With the help of this device, even quite young children can quickly learn to ask questions that probe behind the surface of character and plot, which otherwise they would be unlikely to do. Similar scaffolds can be constructed to ask about aspects of character instead of conduct, about relationships, or about the central themes (the 'Big Ideas') in the book by varying your questions accordingly.

Teachers in the elementary grades will be familiar with the use of question-starters. These are words such as 'who', 'what', 'when', 'where', 'why' and 'how'. When it comes to engaging in ethical inquiry, we need to include words such as 'should' and 'could' among our question-starters. That's *how* such-and-such a character behaved, but *should* he have behaved that way? How else *could* he have behaved? Questions along these lines ask us to think about what makes for good or better conduct or bring us to consider alternative possibilities that may be more appropriate. Extensions to this kind of activity are easily constructed to help students gain more confidence in asking ethical questions, as in the following example.

Activity: I can ask a question

Procedure

1. Write question-starters such as the following on cards and place them in a bag so that they cannot be seen. You'll also need a set of marking pens.

> Was it right that ...?
>
> Is it good to ...?
>
> How bad was ...?
>
> Would it have been better if ...?
>
> Ought ... to have ...?
>
> How else could ... have ...?

2. Break the class into small groups and ask a volunteer from each group to come and reach into the bag for a card and to take a marking pen. Tell the class that they will be asked to make up a question using their question-starter.

3. Read an appropriate picture book to the class—something short and simple.

4. Now ask each group to make up a question about the story using their question-starter.

5. Go around the class and, as necessary, help the groups to write their questions on the cards with their markers. Then pin them up for everyone to see.

6. Tell the class that they will be able to vote for their favourite question. Then read out the questions and have the class vote on a question for discussion.

As students begin to develop the art of questioning, they should learn to distinguish between questions according to how they should go about trying to answer them. They need to distinguish between questions that can be satisfactorily answered by relying on some authoritative source, for example, from those that they need to think about for themselves. They also need to distinguish between questions that permit a variety of responses with little or no need for justification and those that they cannot properly address without giving good reasons for what they say. Questions that turn on matters of purely personal preference are of the former kind, for instance, while those raising ethical issues are of the latter. The structure below, which I call a Question Quadrant, has proven to be a handy practical device for helping students to learn to make such distinctions.

Question Quadrant

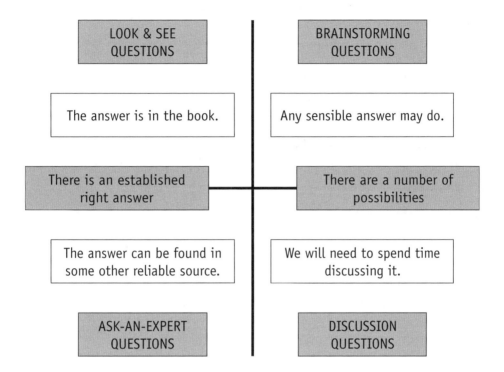

Activity: What kind of question am I?

Procedure

1. Make up Question Quadrant questions of all four kinds in relation to a story that you will read to the class. Write these questions on pieces of card so that they will be legible from across the room. You will need half the number of questions as you have students in your class. (Alternatively, if your students are ready for it, you can provide the materials and tell the students that they will be required to make up their own questions.)

2. Lay the Question Quadrant out on the floor and explain it to the class. Say that you will be reading a story and then handing out questions that they will be asked to place on the quadrant.

3. Read the story.

4. Distribute the question cards, one to each pair of students, reminding them that they are to discuss where their question belongs on the Question Quadrant.

5. When the students are ready, go around the class, having each pair read their question and place it where they think it belongs. Ask each pair to justify their decision. If they are unable to reach agreement or are unsure where to place their question, ask them to give their reasons for this, and then have them seek help from the class.

6. Always check for any disagreement or uncertainty in the class before going on to the next question.

To give the general idea, here are some questions that could be used for the Question Quadrant activity with Pat Thomson's picture book *It's So Unfair!* that was mentioned in the previous chapter.

> ▶ Why did Mrs Prout punish Cat?
> ▶ What naughty things did Cat do?
> ▶ What other naughty things might Cat have done?
> ▶ Why might the other animals have all stuck up for Cat?
> ▶ Do farmyard animals actually tend to get along with cats?
> ▶ Can you train a cat not to do the kinds of things that Cat did?
> ▶ What would have been a fair punishment for Cat given all the naughty things it did?
> ▶ Was it fair of Farmer Prout to send Cat out for what it did to his chair when he had let it back in after it had done all the other naughty things?

It is worth introducing even senior students to the Question Quadrant in order to get them thinking about the character of different kinds of questions. Here is a set of questions relating to an eyewitness account of the stoning to death of two people in Jeddah in 1958, written by RM Macoll (in Carey 1987, pp. 666–667).

> ▸ Who gave the signal for the crowd to start stoning the woman?
> ▸ Why didn't the crowd hear the cries of the executed woman?
> ▸ Where is Jeddah?
> ▸ Is stoning still carried out in Jeddah today?
> ▸ Were the executions carried out under Islamic law?
> ▸ What might have happened if a horrified European were to voice disapproval of the woman's treatment?
> ▸ What do you think would have been going through the woman's mind as she slowly met her death?
> ▸ Is there anything that could possibly justify such unequal treatment between the man and the woman?
> ▸ Should we condemn such executions no matter where or when they were carried out?
> ▸ Would it be right for members of the crowd in Jeddah to condemn the comparative leniency that we show towards people like the man and the woman who they stoned to death?

The teacher as questioner

As a facilitator of ethical inquiry, your engagement with questions and questioning provides a model for students. Unless you adopt a questioning outlook, the students cannot be expected to do so. When we looked at the student as a questioner, we confined ourselves to *substantive questions* relating to the topic under discussion. While I will have more to say on that score, it is vital to recognise that you will need to employ a quite different range of questions to ensure that students attend to the many things that are required to keep the inquiry focused and help it unfold in an orderly fashion. This includes asking students to clarify what they say, to justify their claims, provide examples, consider implications, and so forth. In contrast to the questions into which we inquire, these questions direct us to make certain moves as the inquiry proceeds. We may call them *procedural questions*. Just as you can assist students to learn to probe problems and issues by introducing appropriate topic questions and teaching students to do the same, your use of procedural questions serves not only the needs of that particular inquiry, but provides a model for students to emulate. As procedural questioner, you have one eye on the moment-to-moment needs of the ongoing inquiry and the other eye on developing the students' procedural questioning skills. Let us look a little more closely at the teacher's use of these two types of question: substantive and procedural.

Substantive questions: Constructing Discussion Plans

When conducting discussion, it is usually appropriate to have prepared some questions in advance. These may form an extension to questions that students have already raised in an earlier lesson, they may be designed to ensure that certain aspects of a topic are covered or they merely act as prompts to refocus discussion or rekindle it when things begin to flag. Whatever their specific purpose, it is ill-advised to enter into such a complex activity as the discussion of an ethical concept, issue or problem without having set down some appropriate topic questions. A set of these questions is what we may call a Discussion Plan.

Although Discussion Plans can vary in all kinds of ways, an elementary distinction can be made between ones that are more or less sequential and ones that are not. A sequential Discussion Plan is a series of questions in which each question builds upon those that came before. Such questions are therefore meant to be treated in order. A consecutive set of questions may proceed from the specifics of a text or other stimulus to a broader or more comprehensive consideration of some problem or issue. It may start from things that are already familiar to students and then connect up their experience with things they are only just beginning to explore. Or it may begin with questions that admit of a relatively simple or clear-cut answer and advance to ones where the going is more difficult or uncertain. All such Discussion Plans differ from those where the questions that you have devised could be asked in any order. The order may not be important when the questions circle around a topic so that we can view it from different angles; where they are meant to elicit the consideration of alternative possibilities; designed to highlight a number of related concerns; used to help uncover a cluster of criteria that govern the application of a concept; or are simply meant to bring a number of considerations into play.

Discussion Plans are meant to help provide structure and direction in discussion and may be designed to direct students' attention to a particular aspect of an issue or possible solution to a problem. Raising some questions that are directive in this sense is distinct from constructing a set of questions that attempt to force students to a predetermined conclusion. That is coercive and runs contrary to the spirit of ethical inquiry. Of course, an individual question might be constructed to lean in a particular direction and juxtaposed with another that raises alternative or contrary possibilities. Leading questions can legitimately be used to problematise an issue, but not to corral discussion.

Allow me to flesh this out with some examples, beginning with a sequential Discussion Plan suitable for the upper primary school years. The stimulus for this example is a photograph of a featherless chicken that has been bred for the chicken industry.[2] The beauty of the featherless chicken is that you don't have to pluck it! So other things being equal, that's a saving of time and money. Still, most of us are likely to feel uncomfortable when we look at the image of the featherless chicken. Whether we feel amazement, disgust or pity, it doesn't look as we expect a chicken to look. Do these feelings show that it is wrong to breed featherless

---

2   Images of the featherless chicken and short discussion pieces about it are readily available on the internet. See for example <http://www.nextnature.net/2006/10/featherless-chicken/>.

chickens? Or might we be led astray by our feelings into thinking that something is wrong when it really isn't wrong? The accompanying set of questions provides a basis for students to discuss whether there really is anything wrong with breeding featherless chickens, or sufficiently wrong that we shouldn't do so, while assisting them to think more generally about the role of both feelings and reasons in ethical decision-making.

Discussion Plan: The featherless chicken

1. What do you feel when you look at the featherless chicken?
2. Do those feelings tell you that there is something wrong with breeding featherless chickens?
3. Are our feelings generally a good guide to what is right and wrong?
4. Can our feelings sometimes be mistaken and make us feel that something is wrong when it isn't really wrong?
5. If people feel differently about something, how can we tell who is right?
6. Are there other ways in which we can decide whether something is alright or not, aside from the feelings that we have about it?
7. What reasons can you give for thinking that there is something wrong with breeding featherless chickens?
8. What benefits could we derive from breeding featherless chickens?
9. Are the reasons against breeding featherless chickens sufficiently important to outweigh any possible benefits of breeding them, or not?

The following sequential Discussion Plan was stimulated by another photograph, this time one depicting the living conditions of a family of landless farmers in South Africa's Eastern Cape (Pilger 2001, p. 75). Any number of images readily available on the internet could serve the same purpose. The questions are designed to help students explore ethical issues surrounding poverty. They begin by asking students to conceptualise poverty in both general and concrete terms, and then explore the acceptability of social and international disparities in wealth and the issue of national and international obligations to address poverty. Finally, students are invited to think about responsibility and action in more personal terms.

Discussion Plan: Poverty

1. What is it to live in poverty?
2. What do you think the life of the people in the photograph would be like?
3. Is it acceptable for some people in society to be very poor while others are rich?
4. Is it acceptable for some countries to be very poor while others are rich?
5. Is poverty in a country something that the country should be responsible for dealing with itself, or should the rest of the world help?
6. Do we have a greater obligation to deal with poverty in our own communities than in other parts of the world?
7. Should you personally feel a responsibility to help deal with poverty in other parts of the world?
8. What could you do to help reduce poverty in the world?

Finally, here is a senior secondary example of a sequential Discussion Plan based on the report dealing with the stoning in Jeddah mentioned earlier in this chapter. While the plan begins with a couple of large open questions, it then turns back to the relevance of feelings that are likely to be evoked in people coming from different cultural backgrounds, the connection between law and justice, and then asks whether there is anything else to which we can appeal to help sort the matter out. Finally, it comes to the underlying question about the universality or context-dependence of justice.

Discussion Plan: Justice

1. Were the punishments meted out in Jeddah just or unjust?
2. What would make them just or unjust?
3. If you feel repelled by the stoning in Jeddah, does this mean that it cannot really have been just?
4. If a Saudi Arabian felt vindicated by the stoning in Jeddah, does this mean that it must have been just?
5. If these punishments were just according to Saudi Arabian law and customs does that mean they must be just?
6. Could there be such things as unjust laws, customs and practices? (What about laws that historically supported slavery or racial discrimination?)
7. If laws can be unjust, to what should we appeal in order to determine whether a given law is just or not?
8. Is justice relative to time and place or is it ultimately universal?

These sequential Discussion Plans contrast with non-sequential ones, in which questions are asked in no particular order. A single example should suffice. The following plan assists students to think about various criteria to which people might appeal in claiming that a rule is fair. Such criteria as equal treatment, levelling the playing field, targeting needs, looking to the overall benefit, abiding by majority rule and addressing disadvantage may be appealed to in one context or another, although no such appeal is guaranteed to be free of controversy. The topic is therefore likely to spark a good deal of healthy disagreement among students and should lead to the thoughtful examination of different cases and potential counterexamples.

Discussion Plan: What makes a rule fair?

▶ Are rules fair if they treat everyone alike?

▶ Are rules fair if they handicap people who have a natural advantage?

▶ Are rules fair if they distinguish between people according to their needs?

▶ Are rules fair if they aim at the greatest overall happiness of those who are supposed to abide by them?

▶ Are rules fair if they are accepted by the vast majority of people?

▶ Might a rule be fair if it favoured a group because that group was discriminated against in the past?

I should issue a word of warning about working up Discussion Plans from materials such as narratives. One does not have to go to novels in the senior secondary school English class to encounter the complexities of narrative. Even picture books are likely to be densely laden with concepts, themes and issues that would repay ethical exploration. To take an example almost at random, consider Pamela Allen's classic story *Herbert and Harry* (2000). Here are some of the topics that might come up: cooperation and conflict; luck and good fortune; selfishness; arguments; loneliness; being defensive; fear of loss; fear of others; becoming obsessed by things; making good decisions in life; the connection between what we do and what we become; and what makes for a good life. You could spend a proverbial month of Sundays constructing Discussion Plans for everything that might come up, and while that could be an enjoyable and even enlightening exercise, it isn't practicable when it comes to lesson planning. You would be far better off devoting the first lesson to reading the book, gathering questions from students and deciding with the class which one or ones you will tackle. By reserving discussion for a subsequent lesson, you will have the opportunity to go away and build your supplementary questions around whatever has been selected. Unlike the herculean labour imagined a moment ago, that task is manageable.

To finish, let's look at Discussion Plans for a couple of themes from *Herbert and Harry*. In the story, Herbert and Harry argue about who owns a treasure that gets caught in their fishing net. Herbert maintains that it was his because he pulled it up, while Harry argues that it is his because he chose the place where they cast their net. Arguments of this kind are common, and not only among children. People do not agree about something and each person thinks that they have reasons which justify their own opinion. While there is likely to be some justification in the reasons that people give, self-interest and an unwillingness to honestly weigh other people's interests and reasons against one's own can be a source of escalating conflict. The following Discussion Plan has been designed to help students explore this issue.

Discussion Plan: Settling arguments

▶ Why did Herbert and Harry argue about the treasure that was caught in their net?

▶ When Herbert argued that he should keep the treasure, what reason did he give? And what reason did Harry give for keeping the treasure himself?

▶ Was one of these reasons as to who should keep the treasure a much better reason than the other?

▶ When two people both have a claim to something, how should they go about sorting out what to do?

▶ Is there anything wrong with sorting out our disagreements by *arguing* with one another?

▶ Is there anything wrong with sorting out our disagreements by *fighting* one another?

▶ When you have a disagreement with someone, could you work out what to do by imagining that, for all you know, you might be the other person?

Notice that the first part of the Discussion Plan sets up the theme by locating it in relevant details of the text. Then the discussion becomes more general, asking us to evaluate some of the ways in which we may try to settle arguments. Finally, a strategy is suggested for our consideration. This idea was suggested to me by a famous modern work on justice by the American political philosopher John Rawls (2005).

To take up a second theme, when Herbert and Harry were young, they lived together and had much the same life. After Herbert made off with the treasure, however, their ways parted, and they ended up living very different kinds of lives. Most students would say that, although poorer, Harry lived a better life than Herbert, and could probably give good reasons why they think that is so. This could provide a starting point for thinking more deeply about what makes one kind of life better than another. The first question below, followed by a selection of the others, could help to structure the discussion.

Discussion Plan: A better life

▸ Who do you think lived the better kind of life, Herbert or Harry?
▸ Do you think that your life would probably be better if you came into a fortune?
▸ Would it be better in life to have valuable possessions that you needed to safeguard, or not to have them?
▸ Could it be possible for someone to live a better life by going away and living entirely on their own?
▸ How important are other people in our own efforts to live a better life?
▸ Would your life be better if you had your own family when you grew up?
▸ Would it be better to live in the same place all your life or to move from one place to another throughout your life?
▸ Do you think that whether a person lives a better or worse life could depend upon nothing more than good or bad luck?

▶ Do you think that whether a person lives a better or worse life all depends upon what kind of person they are?

I have included this Discussion Plan as an illustration of one that begins with the characters from the story as though it were going to be sequential, but then proceeds to an assortment of questions that, while they mirror various elements of the story, are of a more general kind and are presented in no particular order.

Finally, although it may be obvious, a Discussion Plan does not need to be formally laid out as a set of questions. In the following example of a non-sequential plan, the same question is being asked about each set of options which students are asked to choose between.

Discussion Plan: Thinking about choices

If you had to choose, which of the following alternatives would you prefer and why would you do so?

▶ Having a brother or sister or being an only child
▶ Doing things with your brother or sister or doing them by yourself
▶ Finding a treasure or making your own fortune
▶ Being carefree but poor or being rich but worried
▶ Having a family when you grow up or not having one
▶ Having lots of children or having lots of money
▶ Being Herbert or being Harry.

Procedural questions: Prompting moves in discussion

As indicated above, there are many reasons why teachers need to ask procedural questions in conducting discussion. The following are some of the more common types of questions that you will need to ask.

Asking for clarification

> ▶ Are you saying the same thing as Amelia?
>
> ▶ What do you suppose Laura means by that?
>
> ▶ How does that differ from what you said earlier?
>
> ▶ How does that help to answer Madeleine's question?
>
> ▶ By such-and-such do you mean so-and-so, or something else?

Looking for other points of view

> ▶ How else might we look at this?
>
> ▶ Can you think of someone who might take a different point of view?
>
> ▶ Is that the only ground on which someone might object?
>
> ▶ Would it be better if we approached this in some other way?
>
> ▶ How about such-and-such? Does that seem like a possibility to you?

Attending to assumptions

> ▶ What are we taking for granted here?
>
> ▶ Is that what you're assuming?
>
> ▶ When Irina says that so-and-so, must she be assuming that such-and-such?
>
> ▶ What else might Will be supposing?
>
> ▶ Are we right to make that assumption?

Exploring concepts

> ▶ Why would that be fair?
>
> ▶ Why couldn't you have a robot for a friend?
>
> ▶ What else is involved in being a good friend?
>
> ▶ Why might someone say that a trick and a lie are the same kind of thing?
>
> ▶ Can we say that an action is right even though it turns out to have terrible consequences?

Thinking about reasons and evidence

> ▶ Do we have good reason to think that so-and-so?
>
> ▶ Would such-and-such be a good reason for believing that so-and-so?
>
> ▶ Is that the only reason why it's wrong to do such-and-such?
>
> ▶ Can anyone think of a better reason?
>
> ▶ How might someone try to justify that claim?

Thinking about inferences and implications

> ▶ What does Olivia's statement imply?
>
> ▶ Does that follow from what Cassandra said?
>
> ▶ Are you saying that it *must* follow from what Rahul said or that it *might* follow?
>
> ▶ Is that consistent with what we said a moment ago?
>
> ▶ If we were to accept what Jake said, then would we also have to agree with Abdul?

Dealing with objections and disagreements

> ‣ Can you explain to Phoebe why you disagree with her?
> ‣ Why do you think Kelvin's example isn't a good one?
> ‣ Why is that an objection to what Alex said?
> ‣ Does it mean that Jack must be entirely wrong?
> ‣ Does anyone disagree with what Paul said?

Seeking intellectual cooperation

> ‣ Would anyone like to add to what Sophie said?
> ‣ Who else agrees with Liam?
> ‣ Do you think that Sarah may be right after all?
> ‣ Do you think that Harrison may have part of the answer?
> ‣ Can anyone help Ella?

There is no guarantee that you will always be able to ask just the right procedural question at the right time. In fact, there are bound to be missed opportunities, especially at the beginning. The best strategy is to listen very carefully to what students are saying and to use your own intelligence. If a student says something that is vague or ambiguous, then clarification is generally called for. If students make unsupported generalisations, then they probably need to be scrutinised. If the justification given for a claim is weak, then students may need to consider whether it is worthy of support. In these and myriad other cases, the teacher's judicious use of questioning can help to guide and support the collaborative inquiry process, keeping it on the rails and giving it greater depth and integrity.

You should also be on the lookout for opportunities to encourage students to ask such questions of one another. Students can be requested to ask one another for clarification, to ask whether someone would like to add on to what they have said, or to see whether anyone disagrees with them or has a different point of view. They can request reasons from one another and ask about inferences. If such demands are introduced gradually, and in the early stages you praise students when they ask one another appropriate questions of these kinds, then your students will soon cotton on and reward your efforts with far better discussions than their beginning efforts might have led you to expect.

Conceptual exploration

When one person insists that a lie was just plain *wrong* while another maintains that it would have been *better* to have told the truth, they are expressing themselves within different conceptual frameworks. 'Right' and 'wrong' are categorical expressions, whereas 'better' and 'worse' express comparative judgment. In addition, to say that something would have been *better* is to make a judgment relative to what is *good*, and 'good' is not in the same category as 'right' and 'wrong'. This only goes to show that what looks like a straightforward disagreement can turn out to be conceptually quite complicated. In order for students to begin to deal with such matters, we need to get them used to thinking about the language they use.

Differences of kind

The most elementary way of distinguishing between things is in terms of differences of kind, and in ethics this is most commonly done through *conceptual opposition*. We oppose the good with the bad, right with wrong, being fair with being unfair and being honest with being dishonest. Students need to be made aware of when they are working within this framework, and one way of doing so is to begin with a warm-up exercise when the lesson calls for that kind of conceptualisation. Here is a simple conceptual warm-up for the middle primary school years.

Activity: Dumbbells

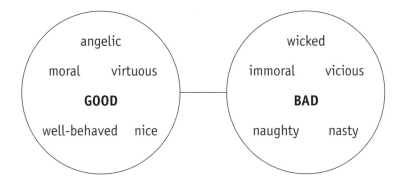

Procedure

1. Write the words for a pair of opposites in the circles of the dumbbell ('good' and 'bad' in the example illustrated).
2. Ask the students if they can think of any other word that is similar in meaning to one of the two words. When a word is suggested, place it in the appropriate circle and see if someone can come up with its opposite. Keep going backwards and forwards until the class runs out of words.

As elementary as this vocabulary exercise is, it provides an entrée to far more complex conceptual exploration, as we will see later on.

Just to take one step in that direction, we can supply lists of words that students are asked to classify. Here is a conceptual exercise with a more sophisticated vocabulary suitable for older students.

Activity: Free or not free?

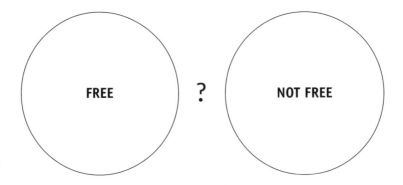

restricted   optional   captive   compulsory   accidental
inevitable   permitted   intentional   voluntary   forced
deliberate   involuntary   liberated   obligatory   trapped

FREE   ?   NOT FREE

Procedure

1. Place cards for 'FREE' and 'NOT FREE' in hoops on the floor and a card marked '?' between them.

2. Distribute the vocabulary items on cards to pairs of students, with the instruction that they need to decide in which circle (if either) their word belongs and be prepared to justify their decision. The '?' is there in case they are uncertain, or cannot agree.

3. Go around the class and have each pair in turn place their card where they think it belongs, and justify their decision.

4. Be sure to have the students discuss any case where their decision is contentious or uncertain.

If we replace the vocabulary list with a variety of discussable cases or scenarios, then the same structure can be used to explore central concepts in ethics, allowing us to examine the criteria that we employ in applying them.

Let us take an example. If asked directly, most students would find it very difficult to say what makes a person morally responsible—let us say, praiseworthy or blameworthy—for their actions. Yet few of them would have difficulty in saying whether, or to what extent, a person is to blame for what happens in a familiar scenario, such as the following: 'Harry didn't mean to knock Melissa over. He was pushed from behind'. Working out why they judge such matters as they do helps to provide criteria for moral responsibility.

Activity: Are they to blame?

TO BLAME	?	NOT TO BLAME

Harry didn't mean to knock Melissa over. He was pushed from behind. Was he to blame for what happened to her?

Najir was supposed to look after his little sister, but he was tired and fell asleep. Is he to be blamed for not looking after her?

Tim desperately wanted to tell the truth but he was too afraid to do so. So could he be blamed for telling a lie?

Jemma was upset that Nicky didn't turn up at her birthday party. But Nicky genuinely forgot all about it. So is she to blame for upsetting Jemma?

Yasmine's new puppy chewed up the corner of the lounge room carpet. She couldn't be watching him all the time. So is she to blame for what happened?

Emily didn't understand that the homework was due today. So can she be blamed for not having done it?

Pete admitted that he shouldn't have left Fang to face the bullies alone, but it was the only way he could save himself. So was he to blame for deserting Fang?

Samantha has a very quick temper and often finds it hard not to lash out. Can she be blamed for that?

Procedure

1. Tell the students that today they will have the opportunity to think about when and why people can be held to be morally responsible for their actions when things go wrong. Then place a card marked 'TO BLAME' and another marked 'NOT TO BLAME' across from each other on the floor of the Discussion Circle, with a third card marked '?' in the middle.

2. Remind the class that the '?' means either not being sure whether the person described is responsible, or else a lack of agreement in their group.

3. Divide the class into groups of four and hand out the scenarios.

4. Tell the groups that they are going to try to decide whether the person in their scenario is to blame for what happens or not, and why. If the members of a group cannot agree among themselves, they will need to explain what reasons pulled them in different directions.

5. Give the students a few minutes to discuss their scenarios.

6. Draw up two columns on the board, one labelled 'TO BLAME' and the other 'NOT TO BLAME'.

7. Stop the small group discussion. When everyone is paying attention, call upon a group where there was agreement that the person in their scenario was not to blame for what happened. Ask someone from that group to read out their scenario and another person to give the group's reasons. Have them place their card where it belongs and record the main point(s) on the board.

8. Now call upon a group where it was agreed that the person was to blame. Ask them to read their scenario, give their reasons and put out their card. Record the main point(s).

9. Go around the circle, asking the other groups to read out their scenarios and place their cards where they think they belong. Ask each group to briefly state the reasons for its decision as you proceed, and record the reasons as before. Don't allow other members of the class to intervene at this stage.

10. Introduce a Speaker's Ball and if you have a scenario that is under the '?' ask whether there is anyone who can help to sort it out. If there are no such cases, then ask those who disagree with where a card has been placed to raise their hands. Select someone and pass the Speaker's Ball to that speaker.

11. Have the students continue the discussion of as many uncertainties or disagreements as time permits, adding to the two columns as fresh points are raised.

12. At the end of the lesson, review the reasons listed in each column on the board, and have the students attempt to summarise the conditions under which we are morally responsible for what happens.

Notice that asking whether someone is *morally* responsible for what happens is not the same as asking whether they are *causally* responsible. Harry knocked Melissa over—he caused her to fall over—but this isn't to say that he was morally responsible for what happened. The criteria for moral responsibility to which students may appeal include having certain duties in a situation, a failure to exercise due control, having or lacking the capacity or opportunity to make a reasoned decision and being in a position to have acted other than in the way someone did. Among the things for which we might be held accountable are our actions, our failure to act, the consequences that follow from either action or inaction and even aspects of our character that figure in how we behave. While the set of scenarios that I have used for illustration relate to the everyday experience of children in upper primary school, it is easy to envisage different sets of scenarios that would raise parallel questions about moral responsibility in other contexts, such as in relation to what characters do in a novel, in thinking about moral responsibility for what happens in society or even for thinking about morality in relation to history.

Tips

▶ While it can be useful to devise a scenario or two where it is clear what we should say, the exercise of the full apparatus of judgment requires cases that are discussable. This means choosing situations where students might differ in their responses to them and where a careful examination of the circumstances and consideration of reasons is required.

▶ Students may respond to a briefly described scenario by saying that 'it depends'—and they may be right to do so. In such a situation, you need to ask those students what additional factors should be taken into account or would weigh with them. When they have fleshed out the scenario, you then need to ask why their decision depends upon those factors. The response to that question delivers or points towards their criteria for judgment.

Differences of degree

By contrast with the 'black and white' thinking of conceptual opposition, we often recognise the many shades of grey that may lie in between. This is to say that, in addition to differences of kind, there can also be differences of degree. We have only to think of *better* and *worse* behaviour to appreciate that fact. To see behaviour as only either good or bad is to miss the vital import of better and worse ways of conducting yourself. The tendency of some adults to pretend to children that morality is always an entirely black and white affair underlines the importance of developing students' capacities for comparative judgment.

As we did with differences of kind, it is useful to begin by providing some simple structures for ordering vocabulary. I call the following conceptual warm-up 'Bridge', because it is a platform along which we may travel between opposing kinds. Whether students are using it to distinguish genuine differences of degree or merely placing vocabulary in order will depend upon the vocabulary being used and the sophistication with which they are able to handle it.

It is worth noting that whether we treat differences as those of kind or of degree can depend on our purposes in distinguishing between things. A satisfactory performance may be better than a poor one, for instance, but we may have reason to recognise poor as opposed to satisfactory performances as ones that are different in kind—a pass as opposed to a fail, for instance. In fact, just about any difference of degree might be regarded as a difference of kind in the right circumstances.

Activity: Bridge

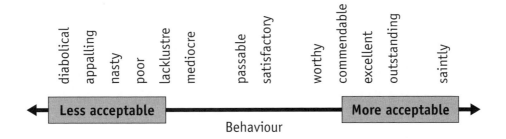

Procedure

1. Stick a line of tape on the floor in the middle of your Discussion Circle and label it as shown. (If you are using different kinds of labels for other material, then be sure that they clearly indicate differences of grade or degree and are not mistaken for opposing categories.)

2. Have a list of words on cards and hand them out to pairs of students. (Alternatively, work with the class on two or three of your examples and then invite pairs of students to come up with a word of their own and write it on a card.)

3. Have the class place their words roughly where they think they belong along the line.

4. Read out the list of words in the order in which they have been placed and engage students in discussion about any reordering that they wish to suggest.

The Bridge structure used above for conceptualising vocabulary can also be used as a support for discussions of ethical concepts or issues. In other words, it is something to build upon. The following activity shows how this can be done.

Activity: Being courageous

Like many morally significant aspects of our conduct, displays of courage admit of degree. People sometimes show extraordinary courage, but they can also display lesser degrees of fortitude without being lily-livered or thought of as cowards. But what exactly is involved in being extremely courageous? And how is showing great courage different from simply being foolhardy? This activity is designed to explore the basis of courage and what distinguishes its different shades and degrees.

◄ **Less courageous** ———————————— **More courageous** ►

Saidu trapped the large and hairy spider and put it out of the house, even though he was terrified of it.	Holly was nervous about the doctor giving her the injection, but she put on a brave face and didn't even flinch.
Although someone might have turned the corner at any moment, Tom sprayed graffiti all over the wall before running away with his friends.	Ahmed is a skilful diver. He's been practising since he was little. He dives from the top diving platform at the swimming pool that most other kids aren't game to use.
Ursula was determined to stop the new girl from being picked on, even though she knew that it would make her lots of enemies in the playground.	Oscar's friends were smoking after school. He was afraid of not fitting in, so he gathered his courage and took a cigarette.
Michael rescued his cat from high up in the tree, which was a very dangerous thing to do, although he didn't seem to think so.	Chloe couldn't stop herself stealing lollies from the supermarket even though she knew that she might get caught.

Procedure

1. If necessary, discuss the difference between an absolute judgment and a comparative one—between what for younger students we may call a 'black and white' judgment and a 'shades of grey' one. (A simple way of doing this is to contrast 'good' and 'bad' with 'better' and 'worse'.)

2. Tell the students that today they will be asked to make 'shades of grey' judgments as to how much courage is involved in various things that people do. Tape a line across the floor of the Discussion Circle and place cards marked 'MORE COURAGEOUS' and 'LESS COURAGEOUS' at its ends. Be sure to make it clear that this arrangement allows for degrees of courage, and doesn't represent two categories.

3. Divide the class into groups of three or four and give each group a card containing one of the scenarios set out on the previous page.

4. Give the groups a few minutes to discuss their scenario and decide how courageous they think it is. Tell them that they will need to be able to justify their decision. Even if they can't agree among themselves, they will need to be able to state their conflicting reasons.

5. Bring the class back together and ask a group that decided its scenario belongs towards the courageous end of the spectrum to place their card there, giving reasons for that decision. Record the reasons as dot points on the board. Do not embark upon further discussion at this stage. That will come later.

6. Do the same for a group that took its scenario to belong towards the other end of the spectrum. Record the group's reasons.

7. Introduce all the other cases, with reasons to be stated briefly. The members of any group unable to agree on where to place their card should be asked to give their reasons and then to place their card off to the side.

8. Now call upon other members of the class to assist any such groups to sort the matter out and to discuss any disagreements about the ordering of the

scenarios. As students enter into discussion and begin to explore their disagreements, introduce the Speaker's Ball. Ensure that it is passed from speaker to speaker to help establish appropriate behaviour in relation to speaking and listening.

9. Discuss other disagreements as time permits, intervening when necessary to keep the discussion focused.

10. At the end of the lesson, have the students review their reasons and recover any general conditions or considerations that make some actions more or less courageous than others.

Once students have a good understanding of what is involved in displaying a greater or a lesser degree of courage, you can ask them not only to give their own examples, but to explain why they are examples of it. They could even use their own examples as a basis of further discussion using the same format as above.

I chose courage because it provides an example of a morally relevant attribute—indeed, a traditional moral *virtue*—that admits of degrees. My treatment of it is meant as a guide to a successful way of constructing an activity of this kind for the purposes of collaborative ethical inquiry. Activities like this will enable students to deepen their understanding and improve their judgment of all kinds of things in the moral domain that are matters of degree. Whether they are considering the extent to which certain social arrangements are just, examining degrees of honesty or thinking about the relative acceptability of various uses to which animals are put, a wide variety of topics lend themselves to exploration of this kind.

Here is an example relating to stem cell research. Senior secondary students studying modern genetic technology could be asked to discuss whether some of these practices are less acceptable than others and why.

> ▶ Harvesting adult stem cells for medical purposes.
>
> ▶ Cloning human embryos to produce stem cells.
>
> ▶ Harvesting stem cells from unwanted human embryos left over from in-vitro fertilisation.
>
> ▶ Producing stem cells by replacing the genetic material in a donor egg with the nucleus of a skin or other cell.

Reasoning

Nothing could be more vital to ethical thinking than drawing appropriate inferences from the available evidence and seeing what people's opinions and suggestions imply. The educational task here is twofold. First, we need to encourage students to be inference-makers. They already do this, of course, but there is a world of difference between the unstudied inference-making in which everyone engages and the disciplined practice of making inferences. We can see this if we consider detectives at a crime scene, sizing up the situation and looking for clues. Just as learning to be a detective involves developing the habit of making inferences, so students should come to see themselves as inference-makers and cultivate that habit in ethics. This requires systematic attention from the teacher. Building on this, the second educational task is to teach students to make *appropriate* inferences. That is to say, in addition to students coming to be in the habit of making inferences when that is necessary, we need to help them to avoid jumping to conclusions and making other elementary mistakes in their reasoning.

Jumping to conclusions is more technically a matter of making unwarranted *inductive inferences*. Inductive inferences are ones in which the grounds or evidence (called *premises*) provided for the conclusion do not give a logical guarantee, but merely offer some reason to suppose that it's true. While the premises of such an *argument* (i.e. a piece of reasoning intended to support a conclusion) may provide anything from a practical certainty to quite minimal support, unwarranted inductive inferences are ones in which the conclusion clearly exceeds the warrant provided by the premises. Students need to be on the lookout for this. Inductive inferences are also widely regarded as underpinning generalisations. Whether or not this is so in a particular case, it is often appropriate to see whether a generalisation has good inductive support, or whether, instead, it is poorly supported or even faces the challenge of significant contrary evidence.

By contrast with inductive inferences, what are called *deductive inferences* provide a logical guarantee that the conclusion is true provided that it is based on true premises—and also provided that, as in mathematics, you don't make mistakes in your reasoning. Such mistakes are called *formal fallacies*. They are 'formal' because the validity or otherwise of a deductive inference depends upon the *form* that the reasoning takes rather than upon extra-logical facts pertaining to the things being reasoned about. We will have space for only a couple of activities that address the topic of formal validity, but that should be sufficient to alert you to the most common errors in deductive reasoning.

Finally, students also need to learn to avoid what are known as *informal fallacies* in reasoning. We will deal with a few of the more egregious types at the end.

Conditional reasoning

Many forms of words indicate that an inference is being made. For example: 'Since ... it follows that ...'; 'Given that ... we can also assume that ...'; 'Because ... we can conclude that ...'; 'We know that ... and therefore ...'. When it comes to inquiry, however, the most natural way to introduce reasoning is through the conditional form, 'If ... then ...'. Even very young students will be familiar with this construction, which has a multitude of everyday uses, such as in promising, warning, bargaining, predicting and planning. In addition, however, the 'If ... then ...' form of the conditional is particularly suitable for inquiry because what the 'If' clause puts forward has the status of a proposition or suggestion, the consequences of which are being drawn out in the 'then' clause. It therefore mirrors a basic feature of collaborative ethical inquiry, which involves drawing out the logical or likely consequences of suggestions in order to evaluate them.

In teaching students about reasoning, it is important to make the form of the reasoning explicit and highly visible. Here is an activity for introducing the form of the conditional in the early years.

Activity: If ... then ...

This activity introduces students to the 'If ... then ...' or conditional form of reasoning which they will later use in thinking about both logical consequences and likely consequences. The idea of logical consequences will become familiar when students begin to engage in deductive reasoning, just as attention to inductive reasoning will help them to focus on likely consequences.

Photograph courtesy of Year 1, Stanmore Public School, Sydney.

Procedure

1. Divide your students into an *If* group and a *then* group, placing 'If' in front of the *If* group and 'then' in front of the *then* group.

2. Begin with a practice run by giving a volunteer in the *If* group a soft ball and asking that person to start with 'If I were to tell a lie ...', following which they roll the ball to someone in the *then* group who thinks they can carry on with a 'then ...' that finishes the sentence. (It is worth having the *then* student repeat the 'If' clause before giving their 'then'. Also ensure that they actually use the word 'then', so as to underline the use of the conditional form.)

3. Ask for another volunteer in the *If* group to start a new sentence with an 'If' for some action that they think is either good or bad.

4. The volunteer then rolls the ball to someone with their hand up in the *then* group as before.

5. The ball is returned to someone else in the *If* group and the process continues on.

Here is a more advanced activity that builds upon the preceding one by taking the consequent of a conditional statement to be the antecedent of a second conditional statement, and so on around the Discussion Circle.

Activity: An 'If ... then ...' round

Procedure

1. Place the words 'If' and 'then' on the floor in the Discussion Circle, reminding students about sentences of the 'If ... then ...' kind.

2. Give a student an 'If' clause (e.g. 'If I were a mean person ...') to be completed with a 'then' clause. Have the student complete the whole sentence.

3. Ask the next student around the circle to use the statement contained in the first student's 'then' clause as an 'If' clause to begin a new 'If ... then ...' statement. (For example, suppose that the first student's 'then' clause were 'then no one would want to be my friend'. The next student would start with 'If no one wanted to be my friend' and complete the sentence with their own 'then' clause.) Make sure that the students actually say 'then'.
4. Continue on following the same procedure.

Note: If a student has difficulty in completing a statement, then ask whether someone can help that person by suggesting a response. Then go back to the student who was being helped. Have the student before them repeat what they said and ask the student who was having difficulty to use the suggestion to complete their own 'If ... then ...' sentence.

Inductive reasoning

As the old saying has it, once bitten, twice shy. While we may have good reason to err on the side of caution when confronted with a situation that has caused us trouble in the past, we should strive to apportion our responses to the evidence and avoid unwarranted conclusions. No doubt our ability to do so is more restricted when we are young and have relatively little life experience to draw upon—we can easily jump to conclusions or overly generalise. This provides all the more reason to alert students to these errors and help them to deal with them when they occur.

Jumping to conclusions

A good way of helping students to learn to avoid unwarranted inductive inference is to have them examine scenarios in which questionable conclusions are drawn. Here is an exercise for the middle-primary age group.

Exercise: Jumping to conclusions

Can you think of an alternative explanation which suggests that the people below may be jumping to conclusions?

1. Tahlia and Grace were best friends. Then Tahlia found out that Grace had begun going over to Mia's house after school. It made her think that she and Grace weren't best friends any more.

2. Jay left his Gameboy in his school bag and after recess it was missing. Angelo was the only person who knew it was there. So Angelo must have taken it.

3. Jessica told Isabel that she had hidden Lachlan's lunchbox. Then she saw Isabel whispering to Lucy. When Lucy saw Jessica staring at them, she made a face at her. Jessica decided that Isabel had told Lucy about the lunchbox.

4. Elizabeth knew that the next-door neighbours neglected their cat. Why else would it keep on coming over the fence to eat from Fluff's bowl?

5. At lunchtime, Zach saw Miss Wilson going out of the schoolyard in Mr Montague's car. They must be in love with one another.

Here is another one for an older age group.

Exercise: What are they assuming?

In each of the following scenarios, you will find someone who reaches a conclusion on the basis of a questionable assumption. Can you identify that assumption?

1. James reckons that Daniel must have sprayed the graffiti on the back wall of the school. Daniel is the only one in the school who would do such a thing.

2. Nicholas was sure that Gabriel was lying about his dad being a policeman. He had seen Gabriel's father being driven away in the back of the police car and he wasn't wearing a uniform.

3. Zoe didn't believe that Riley would keep his word. The only other time she had relied upon him, he had let her down.

4. Hannah was sure that the story being passed around must have come from Georgia. Georgia was the only one outside the family who knew about her scar.

Generalisation

We are sometimes told not to generalise, but that is not sound advice. Clearly, the thing to avoid is *unwarranted* generalisation. Generalisation based on unreliable samples or on very little evidence, *over*generalisation, and failure to look for contrary evidence—these are the things that we should condemn. Insofar as generalisation is based on evidence, it is the product of inductive inference, and when it is ill-supported it is a case of unwarranted inductive inference.

In the area of ethics, we are bound to be concerned with unwarranted generalisations that express prejudice or involve stereotyping. Admittedly, it is not likely that students who generalise about people of a particular ethnic background, for example, or boys who make stereotypical comments about girls have arrived at their views by induction from evidence. Rather, they will have almost certainly picked them up from their social environment and then read them into the particular circumstances in which they express them. Even so, by treating such views as conclusions that are supposed to have some basis in evidence, students can easily show how little support they deserve. Here the search for counterexamples is a useful strategy.

Exercise: Come off it!

Provide one or more counterexamples for each of the following generalisations. (A counterexample is an example that runs contrary to the claim being made.)

▶ If you wear glasses, then you're a nerd or a geek.

▶ Girls only talk about fashion and boy bands.

> ‣ Computer games are just boys' toys.
> ‣ Overweight kids are lazy.
> ‣ Academic types are no good at sport.
> ‣ Sporty types aren't any good academically.

Part of the problem with generalisations is that people often don't bother to make it clear whether their claim is meant to be without exception or whether it merely holds as a rule. When pressed about stereotyping, it is always open to someone to admit that they aren't putting forward a universal generalisation of the strictly 'all' or 'none' kind. In that way, they can try to wriggle out of obvious counterexamples, and still maintain that it is generally the case. Even so, it needs to be pointed out that if someone makes a claim, then it is up to them to justify it. It shouldn't be automatically regarded as true because others cannot prove that it's false. That way of proceeding is to argue from ignorance, a notoriously fallacious move that is discussed on pages 149–50. The best way to confront an unwarranted generalisation head-on is to ask its proponent to prove it. In other words, require them to supply sufficient grounds to make a reasonable inductive inference. Those who make generalisations out of prejudice or by employing prevailing stereotypes will find themselves struggling to provide this evidence.

When thinking about reasoning, it is worth pointing out the logical equivalence of statements of the form 'All A's are B' to 'If something is an A, then it is a B'. So a statement such as 'If you wear glasses, then you're a nerd or a geek' is equivalent to 'All those who wear glasses are nerds or geeks'. By having this pointed out to them and being presented with counterexamples, the defender of such a view is forced into the fallback position, which would be something like, 'If you wear glasses, then you're *likely to be* a nerd or a geek'. This is where the defender of such a claim doesn't get to say, 'Everyone knows that's true' or 'Prove me wrong'. A claim has been made for which we need the evidence. And if we are dealing with stereotypes or claims based on prejudice, we can be assured that no warranted inductive inference will be forthcoming.

In sum, we now have three strategies for dealing with questionable generalisations in the classroom:

1. Is the generalisation strictly one of the 'all' or 'no' kind, and if not what exactly is being claimed?
2. If the generalisation is claimed to be strictly universal, has there been a search for counterexamples?
3. If the generalisation is claimed to be merely the norm, where is the evidence for it?

Generalisations that are based more on presuppositions than on evidence are all too readily taken to be confirmed by incident or anecdote. Such is the nature of bias and prejudice. Yet once we begin to examine them in the light of day, they are shown up for the poorly founded claims that they are. Therefore, we should not be afraid of submitting such unpalatable claims to reason. We should be more worried about the consequences of trying to suppress them simply by condemnation. Reason alone may not entirely drive them out, but it is far better to appeal to and cultivate reasonableness, than to drive such things underground.

Deductive reasoning

Let us now turn to the topic of deductive reasoning. The basic feature of deductive inference is that, so long as you don't make a mistake in your reasoning, if the statements you start with (your *premises*) are true, then the statement that you infer (your *conclusion*) is logically guaranteed also to be true. Here is a middle-primary years activity that can be used to introduce this kind of reasoning.

Activity: So

In 'So' students work out what conclusion can be deduced from a pair of statements.

Procedure

1. Lay out a column of 'So' conclusion cards in the middle of the Discussion Circle, and then give each pair of students a premise card with a statement on it.

2. Tell the students that their statement goes together with a statement that some other pair has, so that you can conclude one of the 'So' statements on the floor.

3. Ask each pair, in turn, to read out their statement and hold it so it can be read by everyone in the circle. Tell the students that once a statement is read out, it should be held up until you say 'Go' and the students place their two statements together alongside the 'So' statement on the floor.

4. When all the statements have been read out to the class, give the students a few moments longer and then, when everyone appears ready, say, 'Go'.

5. Wait until everyone is seated and ready, then go back through their work and discuss any conflicts or difficulties.

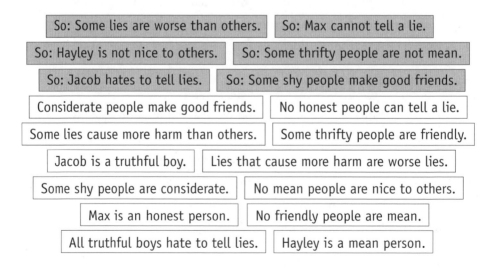

Good and bad deductive reasoning

There are only two ways in which deductive reasoning can fail to deliver the goods. Either one or more of your premises aren't true, or else you make a mistake in your reasoning. No matter how good your reasoning, if your premises aren't true, then you cannot guarantee that you end up with a true conclusion. Our present interest, however, is with spotting mistakes in reasoning. Let's begin with an example from the classroom. The class has begun reading a story called *Elfie* by Matthew Lipman (2003). So far, it is unclear about who or what Elfie might be. Perhaps Elfie is a little girl, or maybe Elfie is an elf, or even an animal of some sort. In discussing this issue, Ruby has come across something in the story that she takes to prove that Elfie is a rabbit. Both Rhys and Tristan disagree. Let us follow them as they discover an error in Ruby's reasoning:

Ruby: I think that Elfie is a rabbit.

Teacher: Why do you think that Elfie is a rabbit, Ruby?

Ruby: Well, because it says here that Elfie curls into a ball to sleep, and that's what rabbits do.

Rhys: That doesn't prove anything, Ruby.

Ruby: I think it proves that Elfie is a rabbit.

Rhys: No it doesn't. What about kittens? They curl into a ball to sleep, and they're not rabbits.

Tristan: I agree with Rhys because I curl up into a ball to sleep— and I am certainly not a rabbit.

If we reconstruct Rhys and Tristan's reasoning here, it seems that they take Ruby to argue as follows:

Elfie curled into a ball to sleep.
Rabbits curl into a ball to sleep.
So: Elfie is a rabbit.

In reply, they show that by the same form of reasoning Ruby would have to accept that kittens are rabbits *and* that Tristan is a rabbit. To take Tristan's version:

Tristan curls up into a ball to sleep.
Rabbits curl up into a ball to sleep.
So: Tristan is a rabbit.

Since it is obviously false that Tristan is a rabbit, something has gone wrong with Ruby's reasoning. Rhys and Tristan provide parallel reasoning in order to show that Ruby's reasoning has gone awry. Such a corrective is a *counterexample*—a term we are already familiar with from our discussion of unwarranted inductive inference. Here the use of counterexamples shows that we have an unwarranted deductive inference.

Here is an exercise that could be used to begin to give students experience in looking out for mistakes in reasoning by providing counterexamples. First, the teacher will need to use the illustration above based on Ruby's reasoning in order to explain what is required. Students could then be asked to do the exercise in pairs, followed by class discussion.

Exercise: Good and bad reasoning

In some of the following examples of reasoning the conclusion drawn doesn't necessarily follow. Can you tell which ones they are? Where the conclusion doesn't necessarily follow, try to show this by inventing an example in the way that Rhys and Tristan did.

1. Michelle said something that isn't true.

   To say something that isn't true is to say something that's false.

   So: Michelle said something that's false.

2. Corey did something unfair.

   Anyone who takes more than their share does something unfair.

   So: Corey took more than his share.

3. Erin raised the most money for charity.

   A redhead raised the most money for charity.

   So: Erin is a redhead.

4. Victoria said something that isn't true.

   To lie is to say something that isn't true.

   So: Victoria lied.

5. An honest person can be trusted.

   Desmond can't be trusted.

   So: Desmond isn't an honest person.

Note: In this exercise, (2) and (4) are invalid. In (2) you can replace taking more than your share with anything unfair and conclude that Corey did that. Students are likely to find (4) more difficult, although the problem is precisely the same as in (2). For lying you can substitute a person's being mistaken in what they say and conclude that Victoria was mistaken. In other words, just because Victoria said something that isn't true, it doesn't follow that she lied, even though that is what liars do. She might simply have been mistaken.

The method of supplying counterexamples is one technique for showing that someone's reasoning has gone astray. The counterexample does this by providing a case where the premises can be true while the conclusion is false. As in (2) above, Corey could have done something unfair, and it can be true that anyone who takes more than their share has done something unfair, while that's not what Corey did. For all we know, he might have done one of any number of other unfair things instead.

As I said earlier, the *validity* of a deductive argument (i.e. that it is logically impossible for its premises to be true while the conclusion is false) depends upon its form. There are two basic forms of valid deductive reasoning that are well worth students knowing about. In order to emphasise that we are talking about the *form* of reasoning, I will present them using letters in place of particular statements that can be substituted for them, and draw a line under the premises to represent the inference to the conclusion. These forms are of considerable antiquity and still go by their traditional Latin names:

MODUS PONENS	*MODUS TOLLENS*
If P, then Q	If P, then Q
P	Not Q
———————	———————
Q	Not P

It can easily be proved that both *modus ponens* and *modus tollens* are valid forms, in that it isn't possible to consistently substitute statements for P and Q in such a way that the premises could be true while the conclusion is false. But since proving that formally would take us out of our way, I will simply rely upon your logical intuition that this is so.

It is common for people to rely upon these forms of reasoning without explicitly setting them out. Consider the following snippet of discussion, for example:

Justin: That guy deserved to be punched.

Georgina: That isn't right, Justin.

Justin: Yes, it is. He punched me first.

Georgina: Come off it, Justin. Just because someone punches you,
                  you don't have to punch them.

In this exchange, Justin appears to be arguing as follows:

If someone punches you, then they deserve to be punched.

That guy punched me.

_____

That guy deserved to be punched.

While I hate to say it, there is nothing wrong with Justin's inference. He is relying upon good old *modus ponens*. If there is a problem, as Georgina suggests, it lies with Justin's unstated premise that if someone punches you, then they deserve to be punched in return. By setting out the reasoning, we can see more clearly that Justin's reasoning depends upon this premise. It also makes clear that Justin's conclusion is unjustified if the premise can be faulted.

By setting things out in this way, we have drawn attention to the *generalisation* upon which the argument turns. This can be important because the generalisations that people rely upon in everyday justification are often in need of scrutiny. As we noted earlier, this is particularly true when it comes to explanations that rely upon questionable attitudes and values. Explanations that appeal to racist and other prejudices provide all-too-frequent examples. For a child to say that some newly arrived student did something 'stupid' because he is an immigrant, for instance, appears to rest on the prejudicial assumption that all immigrants are stupid—a claim that is easily shown to be contrary to fact. (By the way, remember that the generalisation 'All immigrants are stupid' is logically equivalent to 'If someone is an immigrant, then they are stupid'.)

Aside from implicit premises, people can also leave it to others to draw the conclusion. Here is an example that my father used on occasion:

> *Dad*:   If what you're telling me is true, then I'm a monkey's uncle.

Even at a young age, he left it to me to draw the obvious conclusion. In effect, he was relying upon my native ability to reason with *modus tollens*.

> If what you're telling me is true, then I'm a monkey's uncle.
> Obviously, I'm not a monkey's uncle.
> _____
> What you're telling me is not true.

When we reason with *modus tollens* in ethical inquiry we are generally looking for some dubious implication of a suggestion in order to cast doubt back upon the suggestion itself. Here is an example:

> *Joel:* We should always try to prevent harm to as many people as possible.
>
> *Teacher:* Do you mean that it's the *right* thing to do?
>
> *Joel:* Yes. It's kind of like a rule for what's the right thing to do in a disaster or something like that.
>
> *Megan:* Maybe that's right most of the time, Joel, but it isn't always right like you said.
>
> *Joel:* Why not?
>
> *Megan:* Well, then it would be right to deliberately harm an innocent person if that prevented harm to as many other people as possible. Like, it would be right to get an innocent kid into trouble if that would prevent the whole class from being punished.

Here Megan is suggesting that Joel's rule has an unwanted implication—one that she believes is obviously unacceptable—and therefore that the rule can't be accepted as it stands. I will leave it to you to set out her reasoning. It's the kind of thing that you can ask students to do too, as in the following exercise for junior secondary students.

Exercise: What is their reasoning?

Set out the reasoning in the following passages. Which ones involve *modus ponens* and which involve *modus tollens*?

In setting out the reasoning, don't forget that people do not always begin with their premises and end with their conclusion. They may set things out in a different order. Sometimes they may also leave you to supply part of their reasoning—something that they don't actually say but still rely upon in order to draw their conclusion.

1. If you don't keep your promises, then no one will trust you. And that's why no one is going to trust Angus, because he doesn't keep his promises.
2. If Mira was fair to Jasmine, then she would let her have a turn on the computer. But she didn't. So she wasn't being fair.
3. You can't say that Stephanie is a good friend to Joslyn. If someone is a good friend to you, then they don't pass on personal things that you told them about yourself—like Stephanie did.
4. It's true that Aaron views things differently to most other people, but that's what he honestly thinks. So you shouldn't make fun of him.

The two forms of valid reasoning that we have been considering have invalid counterparts. To say that they are invalid is simply to acknowledge that the truth of the premises is no guarantee of the truth of the conclusion in arguments of these forms. They are therefore known as *formal fallacies*.

FALLACY OF DENYING THE ANTECEDENT	*FALLACY OF AFFIRMING THE CONSEQUENT*
If P, then Q	If P, then Q
Not P	Q
———————	———————
Not Q	P

Here is an example of the fallacy of denying the antecedent:

If there's no gold in the morning, then the miller's daughter can't spin straw into gold.
But there is gold in the morning.

_____

So the miller's daughter can spin straw into gold.

Note: While the statements substituted for P and Q are in the negative, and those replacing their negations (not-P and not-Q) are positive, that doesn't matter. All we require is that whatever is substituted for P and Q in the first premise is then negated in the second premise and conclusion.

In this case, the conclusion does not follow from the premises because it is possible for the premises to be true and the conclusion false. As we all know, this reasoning overlooks the possibility that the gold got there in some other way. It ignores what we might call the 'Rumpelstiltskin factor'.

The same problem occurs if we were to argue for the same conclusion in another way:

If the miller's daughter can spin straw into gold, then there'll be gold in the morning.
There is gold in the morning.

_____

So the miller's daughter can spin straw into gold.

Once again, it is possible for the premises to be true while the conclusion is false for exactly the same reason as before. The reasoning is invalid. It involves the fallacy of affirming the consequent. In saying this, it is important to remember that we are dealing with deductive reasoning. From an inductive point of view, the fact that the miller's daughter was locked away all night with bales of straw provides reason to think that she can spin straw into gold. In such tightly controlled conditions, after three nights in a row, we might even say that there is strong evidence of the her powers, providing us with a good inductive argument for them.

As with valid deductive reasoning, it is a good idea to give students practice in identifying the most basic forms of invalid reasoning. Here is a junior secondary school exercise to illustrate.

Exercise: What fallacy is that?

Which of the following arguments involve the fallacy of denying the antecedent and which ones fall for the fallacy of affirming the consequent?

1. If the new drainage system were polluting the river, then we would expect an increase in dead fish. And that's just what we did find. So the new drainage system is polluting the river.
2. If Stokes had an alibi, then he would be innocent. But he has no alibi. So he is not innocent.
3. If the rains were to come early, then the crops would fail. Yet now we know that the rains will not come early. So the crops will not fail.
4. We have a broken window. That's what would have happened if burglars broke in. So we have been burgled.

Informal fallacies

Reasoning can be fallacious without being formally invalid. There is in fact a multitude of other ways in which a person's reasoning may fail to give rational support to their conclusion. Below you will find a list of the informal fallacies that are most relevant to conducting classroom discussion. Apart from alerting the teacher to these erroneous ways of reasoning, it would be well worth students being able to recognise them for what they are by the time they are in middle secondary school. I have added an exercise at the end of the kind that you can find in many textbooks on reasoning, or that, with a little effort, you could make up for yourself.

Ad hominem

When students engage together in ethical inquiry, they need to do so in an ethical fashion. Among other things, this means that there are to be no personal attacks. There is nothing wrong in expressing disagreement with what someone else says, but there is a world of difference between giving reasons for disagreeing with them and engaging in personal attacks. An *ad hominem* is an attack of this kind. It substitutes criticism of someone for criticism of their argument. Suppose that Lily, who is a vegetarian, has just been presenting an argument against meat-eating, and meets with the following rebuttal from Sam: 'That's just the kind of argument that I would expect from a vegetarian.' Sam is not assessing Lily's case on its merits, but dismissing it by attacking her. In effect, Sam argues as follows: 'You're presenting an argument against meat-eating. But you're a vegetarian—and therefore against meat-eating. So your augment isn't worth listening to.' *Ad hominem* arguments have no place in collaborative ethical inquiry, and if they occur then you need to point this out. One way of alerting students to this kind of issue from the outset is to have as a discussion rule that there are to be no put-downs.

Missing the point

In arguing either for or against what someone has said, it is possible to inadvertently miss their point, or even to ignore what's at issue and deliberately argue for or against something else. To miss or ignore the point that the other person has made is clearly to fail to provide reason either for or against the proposition in question. Occasionally students will claim to be responding to someone when in fact they are deliberately shifting the subject onto some related point that they want to make. More commonly, however, they simply misunderstand what is at issue. The following is typical of this kind of problem:

> *Jason*:   Would you tell your little sister that you didn't like the birthday present she made for you even though you hated it? I wouldn't.
>
> *Kylie*:   It would be better to tell her a little white lie than to hurt her feelings.
>
> *Inga*:   I don't agree with Jason and Kylie. You should find something else to say—something that isn't a lie, but that doesn't make her feel bad.

Although Inga's suggestion may be a good one, she has missed the point of the previous remarks. What Jason says is actually consistent with Inga's suggestion, and may be his view for all she knows. She has also misconstrued what Kylie is arguing, which is that telling your little sister a white lie is better than being hurtful by simply saying what you feel. That says nothing to exclude Inga's third option, which Kylie may well agree would be better again.

False alternative

When students respond to an ethical problem, issue or question, they are likely to come up with a range of suggestions. Even so, they may fail to consider some important possibility or, unless appropriate steps are taken, lose track of one or more of their earlier suggestions as the discussion proceeds. This may leave the class arguing about the relative merits of a couple of suggestions or taking sides over some issue, while other relevant possibilities end up being ignored. Even the question that frames the discussion may present a choice between false alternatives. Suppose that the question were: 'Should we morally evaluate a person's action by looking at its consequences or in terms of the intention with which it was performed?' This question raises two important criteria for us to consider—consequences and motive—but it is framed in such a way as to implicitly exclude other possibilities, such as evaluating a person's actions by reference to independent moral principles.

Appeal to ignorance

When students' claims are challenged, they sometimes put the onus back on the challenger to defend their protest. Then, when the challenger is unable to convincingly show that the original claim is unacceptable, its proponent construes that as giving support to the claim. In effect, the claim is taken to be true simply because the challenger doesn't know how to disprove it. That is what is known as an appeal to ignorance. Let me illustrate:

Aiden: It's only fair for you to get even with someone who does something wrong to you.

Anna: I'm not at all sure about that. It doesn't seem right to me.

Aiden: Why not? What's wrong with it?

Anna: I can't really say. It doesn't seem right, that's all.

Aiden: If that's all you've got to say against it, Anna, I guess that I've made my point.

Here Aiden is relying upon an argument from ignorance. Anna has been given no reason to agree with Aiden's claim and it is entirely illicit of Aiden to suggest that Anna should accept it just because she cannot say what's wrong with it. Aiden puts Anna on the back foot, turning the onus of proof back on her. Yet Aiden is the one who made the assertion, and it would have been more appropriate for Anna to ask him to defend it when she found it doubtful.

Begging the question

The fallacy of begging the question arises when an argument assumes the very thing that is at issue. Naturally, there wouldn't be much point in arguing that way if it were plain that it did so. The argument may be formally valid, but it wouldn't prove a thing. Even so, when the same claim is made in two different ways, first as premise and then as conclusion, the circularity of the argument is not always obvious. Here's an example: 'It is worthwhile for students to study ethics because the knowledge they gain will prove to be of real value to them.' While the conclusion that it's worthwhile for students to study ethics follows from the premise that the knowledge gained will prove to be of value, to say that it is worthwhile is simply to say that it is of value, and hence the conclusion is more or less a restatement of the premise.

More often this fallacy arises because the conclusion is used to bolster the argument further down the track. Many people will have experienced this when engaging with an enthusiastic evangelical Christian:

Mathew: The Bible is the revealed word of God.

Claire: You seem very sure of that.

Mathew: That's what God tells us and you can place your trust in Him.

Claire: How do we know that's what God tells us?

Mathew: Because it says so in the Bible.

In this exchange, Mathew is using the claim that the Bible is the word of God in order to argue that the Bible is God's word. Regardless of whether or not Mathew's conclusion is true, or the fact that his argument is formally valid,[3] his reasoning is fallacious.

Straw man

A straw man argument misrepresents the suggestion or proposition against which it is directed. Through exaggeration or oversimplification the original suggestion is turned into one that is more easily defeated, and the argument is directed against that proposition rather than the one that was actually put. Here's an obvious example:

Charmaine: As tragic as it is, I don't see that it's wrong to abort a fetus even quite late in pregnancy when the mother's life is at stake.

Ridley: So you're in favour of killing little children even before they have a chance to be born. That's wrong. How would you like it if someone came along and killed your little brother or sister?

Although unlikely to occur in ethical inquiry in the classroom, straw man arguments can also arise from taking someone's remarks out of context or from deliberately attacking a weaker version of a position rather than a more defensible one.

Straw man arguments are something to particularly look out for when dealing with emotional issues, as well as when matters become complicated. Even though most students are capable of correcting the record when they have been misrepresented in this way, the tendency to attack a straw man needs to be nipped in the bud.

---

3 To all intents and purposes, Mathew's conclusion is the same as his premise. And an argument of the form 'P, therefore P' is valid. It is impossible for the premise to be true while the conclusion is false. Still, this does not save Mathew's reasoning from the charge being levelled at it.

Exercise: What fallacy is that?

Identify the fallacy committed in each of the following passages.

1. You ask me why you should believe that we are composed of three different components: body, mind and spirit. You try proving that we aren't.

2. I don't think that we will ever give up on coal-fired power stations because the alternative to that is to build nuclear power plants, and they're far worse.

3. I don't agree with those who think that it's better to be safe than sorry. I have done some crazy things and I am not sorry I did them.

4. Those who don't believe are damned, because you need to believe in order to be saved.

5. Those who claim to be honest are liars because everyone has told a lie sometime in their life.

6. You reckon that I'm selfish. You're one to talk.

7. She says that you should never mistreat animals. But that's not true. Animals are mistreated all the time.

8. The lawyer for the defence argued that the accused couldn't have committed the crime. I wonder how much he was paid to say that.

9. No one has ever been able to prove that a person's behaviour is simply a product of their nature and their upbringing. So there must be some other factor.

10. Eloise said that you should be able to talk about all kinds of things with your friends, but Madison replied that Eloise was wrong because you shouldn't share your pin numbers with them.

11. If you needed evidence in favour of democracy you only need look at those countries where there's a dictatorship.

12. Allowing everyone freedom of speech is in the interests of society, for the welfare of the community depends upon all of us having the liberty to express our opinions.

Answers: 1) Appeal to ignorance; 2) False alternative; 3) Missing the point; 4) Begging the question; 5) Straw man; 6) Ad hominem; 7) Missing the point; 8) Ad hominem; 9) Appeal to ignorance; 10) Straw man; 11) False alternative; 12) Begging the question.

References

Allen, P 2000, *Herbert and Harry*, Penguin, Melbourne.

Cam, P, Fynes-Clinton, L, Harrison, K, Hinton, L, Scholl, R & Vaseo, S 2007, *Philosophy with young children: a classroom handbook*, Australian Curriculum Studies Association, Canberra.

Carey, J (ed.) 1987, *The Faber book of reportage*, Faber & Faber, London.

Lipman, M 2003, *Elfie*, Institute for the Advancement of Philosophy for Children, New Jersey.

Pilger, J 2001, *Reporting the world*, 21 Publishing, London.

Rawls, J 2005 (1971), *A theory of justice*, Harvard University Press, Boston.

BIBLIOGRAPHY

Allen, P 2000, *Herbert and Harry*, Penguin, Camberwell.

Anderson, E 2010, 'Dewey's Moral Philosophy', in *The Stanford encylopedia of philosophy*, Fall edn, Edward N Zalta (ed.), <http://plato.stanford.edu/archives/fall2010/entries/dewey-moral/>.

Aristotle, *The Nicomachean ethics*, book II, trans. WD Ross, available at <http://classics.mit.edu/Aristotle/nicomachaen.html>.

Bentham, J 2007, *An introduction to the principles of morals and legislation*, Dover Publications, New York.

Blackburn, S 2001, *Being good: a short introduction to ethics*, Oxford University Press.

British Broadcasting Corporation 2012, *Introduction to ethics*, BBC, London, <http://www.bbc.co.uk/ethics/introduction/>.

Bruner, J 1960, *The process of education*, Harvard University Press, Boston.

Burgh, G, Field, T & Freakley, M 2006, *Ethics and the community of inquiry*, Thomson Social Sciences Press, Melbourne.

Cam, P 1995, *Thinking together: philosophical inquiry for the classroom*, Primary English Teaching Association/Hale & Iremonger, Sydney.

Cam, P 1997, *Thinking stories 3*, Hale & Iremonger, Sydney.

Cam, P 1997, *Thinking stories 3: teacher resource activity book*, Hale & Iremonger, Sydney.

Cam, P 2006, *Twenty thinking tools: collaborative inquiry for the classroom*, ACER Press, Camberwell.

Cam, P 2011, *Sophia's question: thinking stories for Australian children*, Hale & Iremonger, Sydney.

Cam, P 2011, *Sophia's question: teacher resource book*, Hale & Iremonger, Sydney.

Cam, P, Fynes-Clinton, L, Harrison, K, Hinton, L, Scholl, R & Vaseo, S 2007, *Philosophy with young children: a classroom handbook*, Australian Curriculum Studies Association, Canberra.

Carey, J (ed.) 1987, *The Faber book of reportage*, Faber & Faber, London.

Cavalier, R 2002, *Online guide to ethics and moral philosophy*, Carnegie Mellon University, Pittsburgh, <caae.phil.cmu.edu/Cavalier/80130/Syllabus.html>.

Department of Industry, Innovation, Science, Research and Tertiary Education n.d., *Logic and values*, M McRae & J Hutson, TechNyou Science Education Resources, Canberra, <education.technyou.edu.au/critical-thinking>.

Dewey, J 1909, Moral principles in education, Houghton Mifflin, Boston. Available at <http://www.gutenberg.org/ebooks/25172>.

Dewey, J 1957 (1919), *Reconstruction in philosophy*, enlarged edn, Beacon Press, Boston.

Dewey, J 1971, 'Teaching ethics in the high school', in J-A Boydston (ed.), *The collected works of John Dewey: early works*, vol. 4, Southern Illinois University Press, Carbondale.

Dewey, J 1980 (1929), *The quest for certainty*, Perigee Books, New York.

Dewey, J 1991 (1910), *How we think*, Prometheus Books, Buffalo, New York. Available at <http://www.gutenberg.org/ebooks/37423>.

Durant, W 1939, *The life of Greece*, Simon & Schuster, New York.

Eshleman, A 2009, 'Moral responsibility', in *The Stanford encyclopedia of philosophy*, Winter edn, Edward N Zalta (ed.), <http://plato.stanford.edu/archives/win2009/entries/moral-responsibility/>.

Fieser, J 2009, 'Ethics', *The Internet Encyclopedia of Philosophy*, <http://www.iep.utm.edu/ethics/>.

Flew, A 1975, *Thinking about thinking*, Fontana/Collins, Glasgow.

Frankena, WK 1989, *Ethics*, 2nd edn, Prentice Hall, New Jersey.

Freakley, M, Burgh, G & Tilt MacSporran, L 2008, *Values education in schools: a resource book for student inquiry*, ACER Press, Camberwell.

Grayling, AC 2003, *What is good? The search for the best way to live*, Weidenfeld & Nicolson, London.

Hume, D 1896 (1739), *A treatise of human nature*, ed. LA Selby-Bigge, Clarendon Press, Oxford. Available at <http://search-ebooks.eu/a-treatise-of-human-nature-258784030>.

Jewell, P, Webster, P, Henderson, L, Dodd, J, Paterson, S & McLaughlin, J 2011, *Teaching ethics: a curriculum-based approach to ethical thinking*, Hawker Brownlow Education, Moorabbin.

Kant, I 1964 (1785), *Groundwork of the metaphysics of morals*, trans. HJ Paton, Harper Torchbooks, New York.

Kelley, D 1988, *The art of reasoning*, WW Norton & Company, New York.

Kohlberg, L 1981, *The philosophy of moral development*, Harper Collins, New York.

Law, S 2006, *The war for children's minds*, Routledge, London.

Lipman, M 1983, *Lisa*, Institute for the Advancement of Philosophy for Children, New Jersey.

Lipman, M 1988, *Philosophy goes to school*, Temple University Press, Philadelphia.

Lipman, M 1995, 'Caring as thinking', *Inquiry: critical thinking across the disciplines*, vol. 15, no. 1, pp. 1–13.

Lipman, M 2003, *Elfie*, Institute for the Advancement of Philosophy for Children, New Jersey.

Lipman, M 2003, *Thinking in education*, 2nd edn, Cambridge University Press.

Lipman, M & Sharp, AM 1985, *Ethical inquiry: instruction manual to accompany Lisa*, 2nd edn, Institute for the Advancement of Philosophy for Children, New Jersey.

Lipman, M, Sharp, AM & Oscanyan, FS 1980, *Philosophy in the classroom*, 2nd edn, Temple University Press, Philadelphia.

MacIntyre, A 1998, *A short history of ethics*, 2nd edn, Routledge, London.

Mill, JS 2008 (1859), *On liberty and other essays*, Oxford University Press. *On Liberty* is available at <http://ebooks.adelaide.edu.au/m/mill/john_stuart/m645o/>.

Noddings, N 2003, *Caring: a feminine approach to ethics and moral education*, 2nd edn, University of California Press, Berkeley.

Norman, R 1983, *The moral philosophers: an introduction to ethics*, Oxford University Press.

Nozick, R 1974, *Anarchy, state and utopia*, Basic Books, New York.

Piaget, J 1999 (1932), *The moral judgment of the child*, Routledge, Abingdon.

Pilger, J 2001, *Reporting the world*, 21 Publishing, London.

Pirie, M 1985, *The book of the fallacy*, Routledge & Kegan Paul, London.

Plato, *The collected dialogues*, E Hamilton & C Huntington (eds), Princeton University Press, New Jersey, 1999.

Pritchard, M 2009, 'Philosophy for children', in *The Stanford encyclopedia of philosophy*, Summer edn, Edward N Zalta (ed.), <http://plato. stanford.edu/archives/sum2009/entries/children/>.

Ralston, S 2008, 'Teaching ethics in the high schools: a Deweyan challenge', *Teaching Ethics*, Fall edn, pp. 73–86.

Rawls, J 2005 (1971), *A theory of justice*, Harvard University Press, Boston.

Richards, TJ 1978, *The language of reason*, Pergamon Press, Sydney.

Richardson, HS 2009, 'Moral reasoning', in *The Stanford encyclopedia of philosophy*, Fall edn, Edward N Zalta (ed.), <http://plato.stanford.edu/ archives/fall2009/entries/reasoning-moral/>.

Russell, B 1961 (1945), *A history of Western philosophy*, George Allen & Unwin, London. Available at <http://archive.org/details/western philosoph035502mbp>.

Sartre, J-P 1992 (1943), *Being and nothingness*, Washington Square Press, New York.

Singer, P 1993, *How are we to live? Ethics in an age of self-interest*, Random House, Sydney.

Sprod, T 2001, *Philosophical discussion in moral education*, Routledge, London.

Straker, D (ed.) 2012, *Questioning*, ChangingMinds.org, <http:// changingminds.org/techniques/questioning/questioning.htm>.

Straughan, R 1982, *Can we teach children to be good?* George Allen & Unwin, London.

Thomson, P 2005, *It's so unfair*, Anderson Press, London.

Weinstein, M 1982, 'Teaching ethics in secondary school,' *Analytic Teaching*, vol. 4, no. 2.

Williams, B 1973, *Morality: an introduction to ethics*, Pelican, Harmondsworth.

INDEX

Twenty Thinking Tools

Philip Cam

Twenty Thinking Tools is designed to support the development of collaborative inquiry-based teaching and learning through class discussion and small group work. It introduces teachers to the theory and practice of collaborative inquiry, and provides an easy-to-follow guide to the tools that students will acquire as they learn to examine issues and explore ideas.

Beginning with an Introductory Toolkit, **Twenty Thinking Tools** shows teachers how to strengthen students' abilities to ask insightful questions, to look at problems and issues from various points of view, to explore disagreements reasonably, to make appropriate use of examples, to draw needful distinctions, and generally to develop their imaginative, conceptual and logical abilities in order to gain a deeper knowledge and understanding of all kinds of subject matter.

The Intermediate and Advanced Toolkits show teachers how to encourage students to make appropriate use of such things as counterexamples, criteria, generalisation, informal reasoning and elementary deductive logic. The Toolkits also include devices for distinguishing between different kinds of questions, for tracking disagreement and for recording discussion.

Twenty Thinking Tools takes students from the early years of schooling right through to senior secondary school, and is illustrated throughout with examples from the classroom, supporting exercises and activities.

sales@acer.edu.au | 03 9277 5447 | Order online: http://shop.acer.edu.au
www.acer.edu.au/publications/education